Contents

Introduction

This book contains 100 imaginative ideas to transform your pupils' learning experience in history by introducing them to the concept that different sources can be used as evidence to investigate and understand the past.

All of the ideas are rooted in an enquiry-led approach. The majority are based on an original historical source and provide suggestions for activities relating to the source suitable for the primary classroom. Thumbnails of the sources can be viewed in the book but high-resolution versions are provided online at www.bloomsbury.com/100-ideas-primary-history along with any transcripts of historical documents. You can print these resources out or display them on your interactive whiteboard as you teach the idea.

The ideas in **Part 1** are suggestions for approaches using sources, which can be used to build pupil confidence when working with primary evidence. These include, for example, employing the concept of 'the mystery document', using 'chat cards' to promote discussion, exploring the difference between fact and opinion, and developing observational skills and awareness of historical terms. In **Parts 2 to 12** the ideas are grouped into source types, which can denote specific questioning, although there are certain universal questions that should be applied to all sources when pupils start to investigate them.

The following sources form the basis of the ideas in this book: photographs, census data, government reports, cartoons, diagrams, posters, police reports, trial documents, seals, manuscripts, maps, and private and official letters. We hope that encounter with such a rich range of source types will expose pupils to the stuff of history and strengthen their skills in handling primary evidence and forming their own interpretations.

The 100 ideas in this book will support teachers in delivering the key aim of the National Curriculum in history: to ensure that all pupils understand the methods of historical enquiry. In addition, all of the sources reflect the primary school history National Curriculum content offering. Therefore, teachers looking for sources relating to such content themes as events beyond living memory of national importance, the lives of significant individuals, changing power of monarchs, aspects of social history from past to present or significant turning points will find useful ideas here.

The ideas suggested are all based on The National Archives collection and are not readily found in existing textbooks. They offer a unique way for primary school pupils to access real historical documents rather than work with extracts published in secondary textbooks. Here, for example, you will find lesson suggestions based on a set of rules for one of Henry VIII's palaces, the first moon landing, a game about Dick Turpin or Nelson's funeral barge, and many more hidden, inspiring stories about the famous and not so famous.

Finally, we hope that the power of working with archival material will encourage you to integrate this approach into your history teaching with your classes and that you will be encouraged to make use of your local archives and The National Archives as historians.

The National Archives

The National Archives is home to more than 1,000 years of the nation's history. As the official archive and publisher for the UK government, and for England and Wales, its role is to preserve official government records for generations to come, and to make them accessible to all. From Shakespeare's will and Domesday Book to beautiful designs and photographs, its unique historical collection is one of the largest in the world.

How to use this book

This book includes quick, easy and practical ideas for you to dip in and out of, to support you in teaching history in the primary classroom.

Each idea includes:

- a catchy title, easy to refer to and share with your colleagues
- an interesting quote linked to the idea
- a summary of the idea in bold, making it easy to flick through the book and identify an idea you want to use at a glance
- a step-by-step guide to implementing the idea.

Where an original historical source is used in the idea, a thumbnail image of the source is provided for reference.

Each idea also includes one or more of the following:

Teaching tip

Practical tips and advice for how and how not to run the activity or put the idea into practice.

Taking it further

Ideas and advice for how to extend the idea or develop it further.

Bonus idea ★

There are eight bonus ideas in this book that are extra exciting, extra original and extra interesting.

To access high-resolution images of the sources used in each idea, as well as transcripts of historical documents, please visit **www.bloomsbury.com/100-ideas-primary-history**. These images and transcripts can be printed and handed out to pupils or projected on a whiteboard.

Share how you use these ideas and find out what other practitioners have done using **#100ideas**.

Approaches using sources

Part 1

The mystery document

'The most important part of a lesson occurs during the first five minutes.'

The mystery document provides an exciting way to get children interested in a new history topic. It involves them in active learning, encouraging them to make their own observations and ask their own questions. The document supplied relates to the suffragettes but this activity can be used with any source.

Print out copies of the document or display it on a whiteboard. Tell the pupils it is an extract from a document and give them five to ten minutes to look closely at it with the following prompts:

- LOOK at the document as an object. DON'T read it. What do you see?
- How was it produced? (Typed)
- How is the text set out on the page? (Dates, short sentences)
- What does this reveal about the type of document it could be? (Diary or calendar)
- When was it written? (No year – just dates)

Then encourage pupils to read the document and make inferences based on its contents:

- Can we tell when it was written? (Consider the language, e.g. *motor, pictures*)
- Can we tell whether it was written by a man or a woman?
- What story does the document tell? (Daily events, leisure and travel, activities)
- Does the diary convey the writer's moods?
- Can you work out what this diary records?

Finally, explain the provenance of the source. In April 1914, two women, Florence Tunks and Hilda Byron, were arrested by the East Suffolk Police. This diary was found in their belongings and a transcript was made. Although appearing as a harmless list of social activities, the diary actually related to successful suffragette outrages.

Is a historian like a detective?

'Historical enquiry is essential for the history classroom and built upon engaging with a range of primary sources.'

Like detectives, historians gather primary sources and interpret them for potential evidence. They enquire into the past, find out why something happened and who was involved. History itself is a constructed view of the past based on reliable evidence, rather like a detective's conclusion about what happened at a crime scene. For both, an investigation includes analysis of primary sources, such as eyewitness accounts, documents or objects, and secondary sources produced afterwards.

Discuss and *define* the words below linked to historians and detectives. Ask the class how both groups work in a similar way. Printable versions of these word lists are available on the companion website to help facilitate this.

For historians
Enquiry questions; explanations; research; primary source; secondary source; conclusion; taking account of different views.

For detectives
Criminal investigation; witness interviews; gathering clues/evidence from the scene; observe [look]; interpret [ask]; conclude; building a case to prove that the law was broken.

Ask your pupils to bring to class three or four sources that show evidence of their early childhood, e.g. photographs, birthday cards, toys, clothing or hospital tags. Explain that these are *primary sources* and historians try to work with *primary sources*. Explain how these differ from *secondary sources,* which, in the context of this activity, could be a book about childcare or a TV programme about childhood today.

Taking it further

Also make a collection of *secondary sources* to clarify the concepts. Discuss the advantages and disadvantages of each type of source.

Bonus idea ★

Stage your own crime scene! Arrange for an older pupil to come into your classroom during the lesson. The 'intruder' removes certain items from your desk. After the incident, give the pupils five minutes to jot down what they recall:

- What was taken?
- Describe the intruder's physical appearance.
- Was anything said?
- What role is the class playing in the situation? (Detective)
- Why do the 'witness' statements vary?

Chat cards

'Chat cards are a great way of getting pupils talking about sources.'

Chat cards are a useful way to encourage exploration of a document and subsequent discussion without too much teacher-led input. This enables pupils to use their observation and inference skills, start thinking about their own questions to ask, and develop their confidence when engaging with primary material.

Teaching tip

Chat cards should look bright and engaging and not have too much text. The idea is to prompt discussion about the documents instead of providing a lengthy worksheet-style activity.

Set a historical enquiry for the pupils and select four documents that can be used as evidence to answer this enquiry. We have used documents relating to propaganda posters during the Second World War, but this activity can be used with a wide range of different materials. You could choose four sources from this book or visit The National Archives education website for more: www.nationalarchives.gov.uk/education. Our example enquiry is:

How effective were posters as propaganda during the Second World War?

Set copies of your four documents around the classroom (one per table) and ask the pupils to work in small groups. Give each group a set of chat cards. They then have about five minutes on each table, exploring the documents and responding to the questions on the cards. Answers can be verbal or noted down, but the main point of the activity is to encourage the pupils to discuss their responses together.

The questions on the chat cards could be:

- What can you see in the document?
- Why has the artist chosen these images?
- What is the message of the document?
- How effective do you think this poster was as a piece of Second World War propaganda? Explain your answer.

Once the pupils have looked at each document, gather them together and ask them to feed back on what they found most interesting about the posters. Return to the historical enquiry and ask the pupils to decide which poster they think was the most effective piece of propaganda, and to stand next to that poster. This is a powerful way to visually gauge which piece of evidence the pupils have chosen, and members of each group can be asked to feed back on their reasoning.

Taking it further

Students could design their own chat cards on a chosen document for other pupils to answer.

Spot the difference

'The experience of looking at sources for similarities and differences can help pupils develop their understanding about change over time.'

Pupils look at two sources to see if they can find similarities and differences and explore why it can be useful for historians to compare different sources on the same topic. This task can be used as a general exercise to build skills in source interpretation within a scheme of work related to the National Curriculum on different aspects of social history.

Print out copies of the two sources (a photograph called *Croquet on the Lawn*, 1872 and a picture showing a women's cycle race, 1891) or project them on a whiteboard. Ask the pupils the following questions:

- What game are the people playing in the photograph?
- Look at the way the ladies are dressed in this photograph. How does it differ from the second source image?
- What is the difference between using a photograph and a picture as evidence of the past?
- Why do you think this photograph was taken?
- In the second source image, look at the bicycles the ladies are riding. How are these different from a modern bicycle? How easy do you think it would have been to ride the bicycles in the picture? Why?
- Compare what the ladies in the crowd are wearing with the ladies on the bicycles. What are the main differences?
- These sources are roughly 20 years apart. Do they show if women's lives had changed in any way? Was there more freedom in women's leisure? Had women's fashion changed? How could changes in what women wore have affected their lives? What other sources could help us find out more?

Making a timeline

'Pupils can use a collection of sources to create a timeline of Queen Victoria's life.'

This task is structured into two parts (Ideas 5 and 6). The first part is designed to develop chronological understanding by investigating three sources that give clues about Queen Victoria's life. Pupils create a simple timeline that they then use to write a biography of Queen Victoria in Idea 6.

You should use three sources for this idea, all available on the website: an illustration of the wedding ceremony of Victoria and Albert (pictured below); a ticket from the Great Western Railway in 1901; an extract from a coronation roll, a document giving details of Victoria's accession to the throne and her coronation in 1838.

Print out copies of the sources or project them on a whiteboard. Encourage pupils to make observational comments based on what they can see and read (use the transcripts from the website if needed). What can they conclude about Queen Victoria's life from these sources?

Look at the sources in turn and see if they can date them and then put them in sequence to create a timeline. Ask the pupils what other sources could help to add information to the timeline.

If your pupils are unfamiliar with the concept of chronology, get them to put a series of events in time or date order. Encourage them, for example, to think about how they started their school day from the very beginning and what they did at particular times.

Writing a biography

'Using a collection of sources, pupils can write a historical biography.'

This task is to write a biography of Queen Victoria based on the timeline created in Idea 5, the sources available for that task and any other primary sources and textbooks you may have available.

Content

Encourage the children to include the following in their biography:

- Personal details: Name, date and place of birth and death.
- Family information: Who were her parents? Who did she marry? Did she have children or grandchildren?
- Where did Victoria live or visit?
- What made Victoria important or famous?
- Personality: What was Victoria like? What did she enjoy and dislike? Who were her friends?
- Important events in Victoria's life, e.g. her coronation, jubilees and the death of Prince Albert.
- What did Victoria look like?
- Was she always popular?

Language

The children should use the language of a historical biography:

- Write in the past tense, e.g. 'Victoria was crowned' not 'Victoria is crowned'.
- Write in the third person, e.g. 'he', 'she', 'Queen Victoria', 'Prince Albert', not 'I'.
- Present facts in date order using the timeline.
- Use quotes and images to back up facts.
- Use time connectives, e.g. 'next', 'then', 'first', 'at the end of her life'.
- Use words that show opinion, e.g. 'I think she had an unforgettable face.'

Numbers in history

'What can a War Office record tell us about Florence Nightingale's requests for hospital equipment?'

This activity encourages children to use numbers to draw conclusions from a historical source.

Florence Nightingale arrived in Scutari, Turkey in November 1854 with a group of nearly 40 nurses from England. Britain was fighting the Crimean War against Russia and the conditions in the hospitals were appalling. Show pupils the source document and ask them to focus on the title. Can they spot a famous name or the name of a place? Draw their attention to the date and the phrase 'Hospital Furniture'. What might this mean? Accept all answers as plausible.

Explain that this is a list from Florence Nightingale of items needed in the hospitals of Scutari (including clothing as well as more traditional items of 'furniture'). Ask them to work in small groups to try to answer:

- What is the biggest number of items needed? Why were so many of these needed?
- What is the smallest number of items needed? What would these have been used for?
- How many bedpans were listed? What would these have been used for?
- How many drawers were needed? What type of item are these?
- What are the three types of basin listed? Why were basins needed in different materials?

Ask pupils to share their findings. Why do they think Nightingale was asked to provide this list? Explain that she tried to source items herself – some donated by members of the public and others by private, wealthy individuals. She had a very good knowledge of what was needed and also had helpful contacts.

Teaching tip

You could break the list into smaller, more manageable sections and give each group one part to work with.

Taking it further

Set the pupils some maths missions. Black out the third column ('Obtained from Public Stores') and ask them to find the missing numbers.

Literacy and history

'How can you use a historical document to inspire creative writing?'

This document provides an engaging way to hook children into a historical theme and inspire them to write creatively about a topic.

Print out copies of the document or display it on a whiteboard. Show pupils the photograph of Henry Munday (without any of the surrounding text). Ask:

- What can they see?
- How old do they think this little boy is?
- Do they think he is rich or poor? Why?
- Where do they think he is?
- Why do they think his photograph has been taken?
- When do they think his photograph was taken?

Now show the children the whole document. Give them five minutes to work in pairs to try to answer the following:

- Can they work out the little boy's name?
- How old is he?
- What type of document is this?
- What has Henry done and what type of punishment has he been given?
- Why do you think Henry has committed this crime?

Emphasise the concept of children being sent to prison in Victorian times, with records showing children as young as seven being imprisoned for their crimes. Explain that Henry's experience is going to form the basis of some creative writing.

Brainstorm what Henry might have been feeling when the photograph was taken and the types of experiences and things he might have encountered in his short life. Where might he have lived? Would he have gone to school or to work? How might he have had fun?

Encourage the children to create metaphors for each of the following to describe Henry Munday and his experience. This could be done as a shared writing exercise or the children could break off into smaller groups. For each metaphor, they will need to consider why they have chosen their particular object and how it relates to Henry.

- A building (e.g. Henry is a workhouse, where people are separated from their loved ones)
- Food (e.g. Henry is a bowl of gruel that slithers and slides, tasteless and grey)
- A piece of clothing
- A season

Piecing the evidence together

'Pupils work with a collection of photographs and documents to practise gathering evidence and drawing conclusions from multiple sources.'

This activity is about getting pupils to practise gathering evidence and drawing conclusions from a number of different primary sources.

Teaching tip

You could give the pupils the map and the exhibit list in turn, so that each group gets to look carefully at each document before drawing their conclusions.

Taking it further

Pupils could investigate other spies (such as Noor Khan mentioned in Idea 30) or investigate the role of spies during the Second World War (see Idea 38).

Explain to the pupils that you are going to give them three photographs to look at. They need to try to work out what they can see in each photograph: who the people are, what they are doing, and when the photographs were taken and why. If the pupils struggle, ask them how the people are dressed and what this can reveal about their jobs, whether the people are posing for the photographs and why, where the people are, and what the background reveals about what the people might be doing.

Then point out the man dressed in civilian clothing. Tell the pupils that his name was Karel Richter and that you are now going to give out two further documents that might reveal a bit more about him. These documents are a map and an exhibit list, and are both available on the website for you to print out. Explain that all the documents have come from the same file and are about the same event.

Give one half of the class copies of the map and the other half copies of the exhibit list. Again, they need to discuss what they observe and then make inferences. What type of document are they looking at? What does it reveal about the people and the scenes in the photographs? Why do they think this is? Does it provide any further information about Karel Richter?

Now bring the pupils back together to discuss their findings. Display large images of both the map and the exhibit list on the whiteboard. Draw their attention to the red writing on the map, making reference to the parachute and transmitter. Ask the pupils what these things are, who might have used them and when. On the exhibit list, draw the pupils' attention to the ration book and ask them to think about when people had documents like this. Also get them to consider the pistol, wireless set and compass. Why did Karel Richter have these belongings? What do they think he was doing? Why has a list of his belongings been produced in a court of law? What does this tell us about what might have happened to Karel Richter?

Once the pupils have provided their feedback and theories about Karel Richter, you can explain the documents and his story in full. Karel Richter was a Sudeten German who had been coerced into becoming a spy by the Nazis. He had tried to escape Germany, had been caught and forced to accept a spy mission.

This was Richter's first mission and he was parachuted into England. He was supposed to be gathering information about another Nazi spy who was suspected of being a double agent. However, Richter was ill prepared for his mission. After hiding for two days in the field where he'd landed, he felt unwell and staggered to the roadside to ask for help. He was spotted by a lorry driver who then reported him to the police. After providing information about his mission to the authorities, and also showing them where he had landed and the belongings he had brought with him, Richter was put on trial for being a spy. He was found guilty and executed in December 1941.

Using historical sources for role play

'Drama is a great way to respond to historical sources and create your own interpretation!'

This activity focuses on the Great Plague of London in 1665 and offers the opportunity for pupils to read and interpret four written sources to create their own historical drama.

Teaching tip

All four sources are available on the website with transcripts.

Taking it further

Pupils could create their own poster to illustrate the plague restrictions decreed by Charles II.

Source 1: This letter was written by Henry Muddiman, a journalist who published newsletters, and gives some figures on plague deaths. The source shows the impact of the plague on a family.

Source 2 (pictured): These are the orders for the prevention of the plague, made by King Charles II in 1666. It shows evidence of how contemporaries tried to prevent the spread of the disease, the role of officials and how people saw the plague as a punishment from God.

Source 3: This letter was written by Thomas Povey, who knew Samuel Pepys and reveals that death was so widespread that many disregarded the heavy restrictions to prevent the spread of the disease.

Source 4: This offers another example of contemporary resistance to these restrictions.

Together, the sources reveal the measures taken by King Charles II in response to the plague and the reaction of people to these restrictions. Print out the sources and transcripts. Break the pupils into groups, giving each group one of the sources. Can they sum up the main ideas of their source in a few words for the rest of the class? Once they are familiar with the content of the four sources, ask each group to draft their own drama reflecting some of the issues, attitudes and concerns of the people living through these times.

The five-second rule!

'It is important to encourage your pupils to develop their observational skills for the interpretation of sources.'

This activity aims to get focused concentration from the pupils and reinforce the skill of looking carefully, by giving them just five seconds to look at a photograph and make observations.

The source is a photograph of a tableau, or posed scene, of the British Empire using actors at the time of Queen Victoria's Golden Jubilee in 1887. Canada, India, Australia and the West Indies were the earliest colonies and others were added during her reign, including New Zealand and large parts of Africa.

Give pupils just five seconds to look at the photograph on the whiteboard then close the image, having asked them to make a mental note of the things they noticed. Discuss their observations as a class.

Then put the image back on the screen and take a closer look. Work with the pupils to understand what this photograph reveals about the British Empire and to decode the symbolism. Provide a definition of the term 'Empire' and explain its expansion during Queen Victoria's reign. Can they describe the people in the photograph? Which countries might they represent? See if they can work out the meaning of the following words in the photograph: *imperator* (a commander-in-chief or emperor of the ancient Romans); *Victoria Regina* (Queen Victoria); *1887* (Queen Victoria's Golden Jubilee); *Dieu* (God). Who is the woman standing next to the shield? (Britannia) Who does she represent? How does she appear and why? Why is the lion included in the scene? (To show courage, strength, power, pride and features of *Britishness*)

Having trouble with transcripts?

'A transcript can help pupils to access a difficult handwritten document or densely typed record but it doesn't always solve the problem of pupils having to digest a lot of text.'

This is an activity to make document transcripts from the original more accessible, especially where the language is difficult or complex. The task is based on a source extract from an article about prison hulks in 1846, suitable for those studying the National Curriculum theme of crime and punishment. By the mid-19th century, prison hulks were seen as places of detention in their own right, rather than temporary holding places for those to be transported to Australia by way of punishment.

The source is an extract from *London Illustrated News*, 21 February 1846. Give your pupils a copy of the transcript for the original newspaper article (you may wish to split it into two parts) and show them what the original source looks like. Ask them to underline the key words in each sentence in the transcript in order to provide just enough sense when read aloud. Alternatively, you could do this at the whiteboard, highlighting the key words on a projected version of the transcript. Discuss the meaning of any difficult or specialist vocabulary for the topic.

Afterwards discuss with pupils what this article tells us about conditions for hulk prisoners. Does it also provide evidence of government attitudes and responses towards punishment and prisoners? Why do they think life was made to be so harsh on board the hulks?

How to make history!

'Building a glossary for the history classroom will really help pupils' understanding of the subject.'

Create your own class record of historical terms to use when learning about the past.

Confidence with the understanding and use of historical terms will deepen pupils' grasp of the nature of the subject. Carry out a class dictionary or Internet search by dividing the class into groups and giving each group four to five words to find out the meaning of.

Ask pupils to record and illustrate the results of their search, which can be used to make an alphabet-style display for the classroom that they can refer to and add to throughout the year.

Words to define could be:

- archive
- chronicle
- decade
- century
- manuscript
- primary source
- secondary source
- historian
- chronology
- fact
- opinion.

Teaching tip

We have provided a suggested list of words and definitions for your glossary in the online resources. You may just want to focus on a few terms at a time or add and replace others.

Taking it further

Create a word search or crossword to reinforce the vocabulary you want your pupils to become confident in using. Alternatively, you could 'adopt' a different word each day or have a word of the week.

Causation: big and little causes

'All causes are beginnings...'

Causation appears simple; it is a way in which to describe how different events relate to one another. However, it is far from simple and is a very difficult concept for pupils to grasp. This document activity starts to explore the relationship between cause and effect.

Use this document: Statement of Claim and Verdict in the case of Ryan v. the Oceanic Steam Navigation Co. Ltd, 30 June 1912. Print out copies or display it on a whiteboard. Don't say anything about it at this point. Just give the pupils five to ten minutes to look closely at the document and to start making their own observations. Can they start to answer some of the 'W' questions about the document? What? Who? When? Where? Why?

Encourage the pupils to work out what type of document this is, the date it was created and why Thomas Ryan is suing the Oceanic Steam Navigation Co. (the White Star Line). Explain that Thomas Ryan is the father of Patrick Ryan, a cattle-dealer who perished on board the Titanic. His father is suing the White Star Line as Patrick supported his father and, since his death, Thomas has had no means of support.

Ask the pupils to look at the section entitled 'Particulars of Negligence'. Can they work out what this term means? Ask them to skim-read the paragraph below the heading (this can be done as a paired activity). Have they now got any further ideas about what this term means? Explain that 'Particulars of Negligence' refers to the different causes that Thomas Ryan believes led to the loss of life on board the Titanic.

Ask the pupils to highlight each of the causes. How many causes can they find in total? Can they explain what each of the causes means? Pupils could now start to categorise the causes using the different stages of the Titanic's journey. Provide them with a simple table that has the following headings:

1 Before Titanic sails
2 During the voyage
3 After Titanic hits ice

These headings cover the background and contextual causes, the medium-term causes and the immediate trigger causes. Now categorise the causes as a whole-class activity. Encourage discussion if pupils disagree with each other and ask them to explain their reasoning.

Once the class have agreed on the categorisation of causes, ask them to think about why so many people perished in the disaster. Which of these was the most significant cause of the loss of life? Ask pupils to explain their answers. You could extend their thinking by posing additional extension questions: e.g. Are any of these causes the *only* reason why so many lives were lost? How did the Titanic's reputation as 'unsinkable' impact on each of these causes?

I don't believe it!

'Why is it worth understanding the difference between fact and opinion in history?'

This activity is aimed at helping pupils to understand the difference between a fact and an opinion. Historical facts are based on a body of source evidence, not purely on opinions of what we think might have happened.

Ask the pupils to jot down a fact about themselves or someone they know. Ask for some examples from the class. Ask how they know their example is a fact. Be clear that a fact never changes and can be checked with evidence or proof; in history we call this a *primary source*. Give some more examples of facts and explain why each is founded on evidence or proof:

- Triangles have three sides.
- Ice melts when it is warm.
- The moon is not made of cheese.

Now get them to jot down or provide an opinion – their personal view on something. Share some different opinions. Give some more examples of opinions:

- Seaside holidays are much better than staying in the countryside.
- Apples are the best fruit you can eat.
- Young children should not be allowed to go into museums.

Now ask: Can you give an example of a historical fact and how do we know it is a historical fact?

If they are not sure, you can explain that historical facts can always be checked out by using *primary sources*. Historians use primary sources such as letters, reports, diaries, photographs, manuscripts, posters, cartoons, paintings, buildings and objects that come from the time itself. They provide original first-hand evidence.

Work through this example:

Fact	How can we check this historical fact?
Florence Nightingale lived in the past and carried out work that improved nursing.	We can see her birth certificate, see portraits of her, read letters written by people who were alive at the same time and who described her work or knew her.
King John sealed Magna Carta in 1215.	We can see the actual document.
Winston Churchill was Prime Minister during the Second World War.	We can listen to radio broadcasts of the time, see newsreel and newspapers, read government documents.

Now go back to *opinion*. Ask the class why history as a subject can contain both facts *and* opinions? This is because historians try to explain why and how things happened in the past and so are giving their opinion or interpretation of the facts. There might not be lots of primary sources to study so they draw their own conclusions about what happened. Therefore, it is important to remember that their interpretations or opinions are based on fact but are not fact themselves. Historical interpretations of events can also change, as more primary sources are discovered about that time.

Bonus idea ★

Make a class display of primary evidence on a history topic. You can use sources in this book or search for more sources online.

Open your eyes and see what you can spy!

'Sharpen up children's observational skills in the classroom with historical objects and sources.'

This activity is about encouraging children to be as observant as possible when looking at sources or objects.

Use this technique to establish the idea that we can find out things from sources if we become really practised in looking. You could adopt the technique of the game of *I Spy* itself when looking at the sources together with the pupils, e.g. 'I spy something beginning with P [photograph]', then provide the pupils with more specific observational first-letter prompts about the source itself, e.g. 'P' for posed or 'V' for Victorian.

Taking it further

Print out large A3 copies of your sources and ask the pupils to annotate them with their comments and observations.

Your classroom can be set up to have a display of different types of sources: posters, photographs, letters, maps, plans and objects relating to a given historical topic. Children then work in pairs and record what they 'spy'. For example: What type of source is it? What is it made of? Can we tell the date or time it was produced? Why was it produced/written/ made? What was it used for? Who would have used/read it? Build in a plenary at the end of the lesson to share what the pupils have discovered about the sources.

This is another way of developing observational skills, language and confidence in discussion. It could be used to introduce pupils to a historical character or topic in history. The activity can also be used to help develop an appreciation of the difference between past and present and of the similarities and differences between historical sources.

What's in the box?

'Understanding what an archive is makes it a great place for pupils to start engaging with history.'

The aim of this idea is to find out the meaning of the word _archive_ and then create your own school 'archive' box.

Carry out a dictionary or online search with your class. Explain that archives are collections of information that are called records. They can be letters, manuscripts, reports, posters, cartoons, maps, photographs, films or even sound recordings.

Create your own archive box on the history of your school. Collect together different sources. Your school may have its own archive material, including school logbooks, registers, photographs, objects, timetables and letters. Tell the pupils about The National Archives.

The National Archives is the largest archive in the United Kingdom, but there are many other, smaller archives all over the country. The National Archives looks after the UK government's documents, which go back over 1,000 years from William the Conqueror's Domesday Book to the present. Famous documents held include a version of Magna Carta, Shakespeare's will, Guy Fawkes' confession and Elizabeth I's Great Seal. The archive holds over 14 million documents on shelving that grows by a mile each year as it receives more documents to look after.

Taking it further

Visit your local archive, local history studies centre or library. Look at their website for the type of primary sources available. Contact a local museum to offer context for the documents collected for the archive box. Museum handling boxes may be available.

Working with captions

'How can words change a picture's meaning?'

Photographs can be manipulated, the images doctored or changed. This capability was available at the time of the Second World War, but the Ministry of Information also realised how a simple caption can control how a photograph is interpreted. This activity helps pupils to understand the power of propaganda.

Display the photograph of the munitions factory on the whiteboard. Ask pupils for their observations and inferences. Where and when has this photograph been taken? Who are the people and what are they doing? Explain that this photograph shows female workers in a British munitions factory during the Second World War.

Next reveal this caption alongside the photo: *Desperate British turn to housewives for help!* Ask the pupils to think again about what the photograph reveals. Who might have used this photograph and caption, and why? Then replace the caption with: *Mum is helping the war at home!* How do the pupils interpret the photograph now?

Explain that the Ministry of Information during the Second World War was responsible for propaganda and censorship. Propaganda was a way of persuading people to think or behave in a certain way, often by portraying a skewed view or only part of a story in film, posters and photographs. Captions could have a powerful effect on how images were interpreted.

Now split the class in two and give them the remaining two images available on the website. Tell one half they are working for the Ministry of Information in Britain during the Second World War. Tell the other half they are working for the Nazi equivalent in Germany. Ask them to write a caption for each image to turn them into propaganda for their respective governments!

GIRLS GO TO IT. GIRLS PRODUCING SHELLS AT A MINISTRY OF SUPPLY FACTORY SOMEWHERE IN ENGLAND.

11. A girl fitting caps to finished shells ready for despatch, which will now be filled.

Photographs

Part 2

Is it true that the camera never lies?

'Photographs are a great way for children studying history to find out about the past.'

This activity is about using photographs from Victorian times when people first started to take photographs with simple cameras. Photographs are a fun way to get children to engage with sources without having the difficulty of text. They provide an important means of developing observational skills and appreciation of the difference between past and present or similarity and difference. Working with photographs is also good for developing confidence in language skills.

Taking it further

Ask the children to take their own photographs, some posed and others not. Discuss why posing creates a different type of photograph and how this might influence what a historian can find out about the past.

To establish the idea that we can find out things from photographs and to get children practised in looking, start this activity by sharing different photographs in groups and letting children talk about what they can see. Photographs can be a wide selection from magazines, books, old school class photographs and some provided by the children themselves.

Then use the photograph: The Duchess of Albany with young Duke and other children with rocking-horse, 1891. Print out copies or project the photograph on a whiteboard. Encourage pupils to make observational comments based on who and what they see. Ask them to describe the content, appearance and where the photograph has been taken. Then encourage pupils to become more analytical in order to make sense of their observations. Is the photograph posed in any way? Why might this photograph have been taken? Who could have been the audience for it? Ask them to draw some conclusions: what does this show about play, types of toys, clothing or childhood, for example?

More fun with photographs

'It is surprising the amount of information pupils can draw from a photograph.'

This is another activity using a Victorian photograph but with a difference, owing to the addition of a caption, which adds to our interpretation of the source.

Use this source: Photograph of a man, his wife and two daughters, 1887. Print out copies of the photograph or project it on a whiteboard. Encourage pupils to make observational comments based on who and what they see. Ask them to look at each individual in the photograph and describe the role they seem to play in the composition itself. Why might this photograph have been taken?

Ask pupils to draw some conclusions about what the photograph shows about the roles of men and women, dress, class, childhood or education. Would other Victorian photographs showing families help us find out more about their lives in the past?

Tell the pupils that the original caption supplied with the source is *Industry and thrift*. Define these words. Then open up a discussion as to why a caption is important to a historian. It can reveal the message of a source. In this case, the caption puts into words that the family *wanted* to appear hard working and not extravagant – important values held at that time. The composition strengthens its testimony to Victorian values.

Taking it further

Ask the pupils to write their own character description of any of the people shown in this historical photograph.

27

Airbrushed out of history

'How did the government manipulate images of the suffragettes?'

Photographs are able to capture a moment in time, whereas the same scene would need many words to convey its sense. However, they should be treated with the same caution as any other type of historical source. This activity demonstrates how photographs can be manipulated, but at the same time, how this 'manipulation' can reveal a lot about the people and the society who created them.

Show the pupils the photograph of Evelyn Manesta on the whiteboard. Get the pupils to make as many observations as they possibly can about the image in 60 seconds. You can display the timer on the whiteboard as you do this, to help them focus their ideas! List the pupils' suggestions on the board, before using a different-coloured pen to record their inferences. Remind the pupils that inferences need to be based on their observations, e.g. 'The person in the photograph is wearing a coat, so I think the weather must have been cold when the image was taken.' Guide the pupils with their inferences, asking them questions: Who do you think this person is? Where do you think this person is? When and why do you think this photograph has been taken?

If the pupils haven't already made the observation and associated inferences, draw their attention to the expression on Manesta's face and the arm around her neck. What inferences can they make about these observations? Why is the arm there? Why do they think Manesta has this expression on her face? At this point, accept all answers as plausible and record them on the board.

Now give the pupils copies of the Scotland Yard memo. Explain that this next document might help them work out a little bit more about the photograph they've just looked at. Get the pupils to work in small groups and read the highlighted text. Tell them not to worry about understanding every word, but see if they can work out what type of document it is and the date of the document. Who do they think Manesta is? What has she done? Is there anything else they notice about the document?

Display the memo on the whiteboard and bring the class back together to share their findings. Start with the type of document and what this means, and the date it was produced, before going on to take suggestions about who Manesta is. The pupils may have already noticed the doctored photograph at the bottom of the page. If they haven't, draw their attention to it. Where have they seen this photograph before? How is it different? Why might this image have been altered? What does this tell us about the people who made the document and what they were worried about?

Once the pupils have given their suggestions, explain that you will now reveal the mystery! Tell them about Evelyn Manesta, her role as a suffragette and how she was imprisoned for damaging works of art in a Manchester art gallery. You could ask the pupils why suffragettes might have employed this type of tactic.

Explain that Manesta (along with other suffragettes in prison) had their photographs taken. These were kept on file by the government and circulated between the authorities across the country. Manesta had refused to have her photograph taken, which was why a warden was required to hold her in place, why she hid her hands in her pockets and why she attempted to disguise her face as much as possible. Get the pupils to think about why the original image was not used by the government, and why they went to great lengths to manipulate the photograph and paint out the hand around Manesta's neck. What does this tell us about the government and their concerns about the suffragette movement?

Show us your holiday photos!

'You can use an old photograph to find out about Victorian leisure.'

In Victorian times the only holidays people had were Christmas Day, Boxing Day and Easter Monday, plus four bank holidays added in 1871. As rail transport improved people took trips to the seaside. Seaside towns such as Blackpool and Brighton became popular for sea bathing, boating, donkey riding, and visiting the circus, musical halls and Punch and Judy shows. Wealthy people used bathing machines to change into their bathing costumes and enter the sea.

Teaching tip

To start, the class could look at several seaside pictures from today or even study one of Bognor now. Discuss with the children what they do on a seaside holiday and where they go.

Taking it further

Build up a collection of photographs of different Victorian seaside locations by carrying out a web search of, for example, Brighton, Blackpool, Southend, Ventnor, Hastings and Scarborough. Plot their locations on a map of Britain.

The source for this activity is a photograph showing the seaside and esplanade at Bognor in 1884. Print out copies of the photograph or project it on a whiteboard. Define *esplanade* (used in the caption) as a long, open, level area, typically beside the sea, along which people may walk for pleasure in front of the buildings.

Ask the pupils what they can see in the photograph. Have they noticed the large buildings? (Hotels) Have they spotted the bathing machines? What are they used for? How are people dressed on the beach? Is this surprising? Is anybody sunbathing? What would it have been like to visit the beach clothed in this way? (Restricted, quite formal, sea bathing rather than swimming) How can we find out more about the Victorian seaside? (See other photographs, newspapers or advertisements for events) What do you do at the seaside? Where and when do you go? What are the differences and similarities between your holiday and a Victorian seaside holiday?

Working with feathers?

'Use a photograph to show changes in the world of work in history.'

This photograph is an interesting source for pupils because it offers the opportunity to discuss changes in the world of work and children's education from the 19th century. It also provides the chance to explore with the pupils some of the advantages and disadvantages of photographs as sources.

Use the photograph: Boy plucking a duck, 1886, titled *Keeping Mother*. Print out copies or project it on a whiteboard. Ask the children: What are you looking at? What is this boy doing? How old do you think he is? Is there anything surprising about the way he is dressed? (Quite formal, uncomfortable clothes for a young boy and no protective clothing) Is this a job children might do today? What would it be like to do this work? What else can we learn from the photograph? (This job was done by hand, not machine.)

Explain that some children worked in Victorian times, which suggests the boy is not from a rich family. Perhaps he is over ten years old because in 1880 an Education Act made school attendance compulsory from the age of five to ten, although by the early 1890s attendance within this age group was still less than 82 per cent. Also, many children had jobs after school hours to help support their families.

Ask pupils why they think this photograph was called *Keeping Mother*. What are the advantages and disadvantages of using photographs like this to find out about the past? Why do you think this photograph was taken? What other sources could we use to find out about working lives in the past? (Different photographs, the census, factory and mines reports and records)

Private letters

Part 3

Lost in the post?

'Old letters in the classroom help pupils to engage with the past.'

This document activity uses a handwritten letter to the editor of *The Times* as a source from the 19th century.

Taking it further

The pupils could write their own letter to the headteacher about an issue they care about.

To establish the idea that we can find out things from different *types* of letters, start this activity by sharing examples of letters from today in groups and let the children talk about what they discover. This could include a school letter to parents, a private letter from a friend or a business letter from a utility company. When pupils look at the letters, encourage them to appreciate the difference between *what* is being said and *how* it is being said. They should consider the effect of the language, tone and style used within the letter, and its intended audience.

The historical letter concerns the Great Exhibition that took place in 1851 in Hyde Park in the specially-built Crystal Palace. The exhibition was conceived by Prince Albert to put on show the best manufactured objects from around the world. Print out copies of the letter or project it on a whiteboard. Encourage pupils to make observational comments based on what they see.

Ask them to read the letter (using the transcript if needed). What is the letter about? Why has this man written to a newspaper editor? Why has the author referred to Charles Dickens and what might this suggest? Encourage the pupils to find out more about the Great Exhibition and see if they can date the letter. Get them to draw some conclusions from the nature of the handwriting, style and tone. Does it reveal anything about the author? Was he educated? What does the letter suggest about the Great Exhibition itself?

How to use a 17th-century letter

'Even if the language is different or unusual, it's fun for children to try to work out the meaning!'

This activity focuses on a private 17th-century letter relating to the famous Gunpowder Plot of 1605 and offers a really fun way of getting children to read and interpret a written source. The handwriting is readable but a transcript is available.

Print out copies of the letter or project it on a whiteboard. Start by looking at the form and layout of the letter. Is there an address? Who is the letter to? Who is it from? Can the pupils think why it is unsigned? Is it dated?

Then read the letter together, using the transcript if needed. Define and underline key difficult words: *preservacion* (safety); *concurred* (agreed); *country* (estate); *cowncel* (advice); *no apparance of anni stir* (sign of a problem). Can the pupils sum up the main ideas? Can we tell anything about the relationship between sender and recipient? It is important to encourage the pupils to think about how a letter can show evidence of a particular tone or style or be written in a particular way. Is the letter formal or informal? This can give us clues about the person who wrote the letter and how they wanted it to be received.

Explain that this letter was to Lord Monteagle, an important Catholic nobleman. He gave it to the Privy Council, the king's key advisors. Tell the pupils that the plot failed as the night before the opening of Parliament the cellars were searched. A man called John Johnson, also known as Guy Fawkes, was found with 36 barrels of gunpowder.

Teaching tip

Guy Fawkes was not the main plotter of the Gunpowder Plot, a myth perpetuated by annual celebrations that take place every 5th November. Why do pupils think he is especially remembered?

Taking it further

Ask pupils to write their own version of this letter (a simplified version is available on the website for reference).

Letter from the trenches

'Personal letters are an excellent way for pupils to learn about First World War remembrance.'

The source for this activity is one of many letters sent by staff of the Great Western Railway Audit Office at Paddington who had enlisted to fight in the First World War. William Charles Davies was born in 1884 and joined the Royal Army Medical Corps. He worked in a field hospital in France and fought in the trenches.

Teaching tip

It is important that pupils have some understanding of the countries involved in the First World War and the idea of trench warfare. You could show them contemporary film footage showing men digging trenches in England for training purposes: www.nationalarchives.gov.uk/education/focuson/film/film-archive/player.asp?catID=2&subCatID=3&filmID=3.

Print out copies of the letter and the accompanying photograph (available on the website) or project them on a whiteboard. Encourage pupils to make observational comments about the letter based on who and what they see, e.g. it's written on flimsy paper and in pencil; it must be to someone the author knew well as it starts 'Dear Charlie' and is signed 'Will'.

Explain the context of the letter and define trenches. Then have a go at reading the letter, using the transcript if you need to, and discuss the following questions. What does Davies mean by 'it's a warm shop'? What were conditions like in the trenches? How have the people at home been attacked? Does Davies think the war will end soon? What were taubes? (German aircraft) Why does he not give details about the movement of soldiers in his letter? Do you think Davies would have written a different type of letter had he been writing to his family? What do you think about the tone of the letter? Is it happy, sad or optimistic? Does this source help explain why we remember the First World War?

His last letter

'What does a private letter written to Queen Elizabeth I reveal about her relationship with the Earl of Leicester?'

This activity uses a private letter written by Robert Dudley, the Earl of Leicester, to Queen Elizabeth I in 1588. This was their last correspondence, as Dudley died a week later.

Project the letter on the whiteboard. What can pupils spot? What might the document be? Refer to the layout on the page, with the signature at the bottom. When might the document have been made? Do they recognise any words?

Explain that this document is a letter written to Elizabeth I by one of her advisers, Robert Dudley, the Earl of Leicester. Give the pupils a simplified transcript of the letter and ask them to consider the following questions in pairs: (1) Why is Dudley writing to the Queen? (2) What is wrong with Dudley? (3) Do you think that Dudley and the Queen were good friends? Why? Ask the pupils to feed back their answers. Focus particularly on the last question. How can they tell that Dudley and the Queen cared about each other? (Refer to the 'token' or favour Elizabeth had sent Dudley. This was probably a ring or trinket to show her affection.)

Now explain that Elizabeth and Dudley had been friends since they were very young and it was rumoured they were in love. Even though Dudley had secretly married another lady, he still remained one of the Queen's favourites. When Elizabeth died 15 years after Dudley, this letter was found amongst her personal possessions and she had written 'his last letter' beside it. Ask the pupils why they think the Queen kept this letter and titled it in this way. What does this reveal about her personal feelings?

IDEA 28

Tudor turning point in history?

'How to use a 16th-century document to explore the story of the Armada.'

This activity uses an extract from a letter written by John Hawkins, an English slave trader, naval commander and ship builder. He was vice admiral in the battle with the Spanish Armada. He has written to Sir Francis Walsingham, one of Elizabeth I's main advisors. The idea could be used to teach the National Curriculum topic of a significant turning point in British history.

Teaching tip

It is important that the class are familiar with the story of the Spanish Armada and what happened when they attempted to invade England. This letter shows the real sense of danger faced by the English and also gives insight into their religious beliefs.

Print out copies of the letter or project it on a whiteboard. Instruct the children to look at the letter to see if they can spot any words in the original before reading the transcript. (Read 'y' as 'i' and 'c' as 't' to help unlock meaning.)

Then, using the transcript, read the letter line by line. Ask the pupils as you go through:

- How does the letter suggest the Spanish fleet is very powerful? (Described as *forcible* and the English sailors need as much gunpowder and cannonballs as possible to defeat them.)
- Why do we get a sense the English are scared? (Hawkins says the Spanish fleet is the biggest 'combination' or combined fleet.)
- What does he say about the English sailors? (They need food and wages and the ships need supplies of rope and canvas for sails.)
- How does the letter indicate that religious belief was important to the Tudors? (He mentions *'so praying to god for a hapyed deliveraunce'* and *'with gods favour we shall confound ther devyces'* (plans).)
- Does Hawkins seem confident that the Spanish have been defeated? Why did the English chase the Spanish as they sailed towards Scotland?

Letters from history

'Historical letters can help pupils connect to voices from the past.'

Letters can spark pupils' imaginations and give them an insight into people's actions and emotions. This activity centres on a letter written by Catherine Howard (Henry VIII's fifth wife) to her supposed lover, Thomas Culpepper. She wrote this letter when she was married to Henry and it was later used as evidence of her treason against the king, resulting in her imprisonment and execution.

Print out copies of the document or project it on a whiteboard. Ask the pupils to look at the document for one minute. What type of document do they think it is? Why? Encourage pupils to look closely at the letter and see if they can make out any words. Can they work out who the letter is from and to? Can they try dating the letter? Draw their attention to the signature 'Catherine'. Do they have any ideas about who this person was?

Now give the pupils the simplified transcript. Get them to work in pairs and try to answer the following:

- Who is Catherine writing to?
- Why do you think Catherine is writing to this person?
- What does Catherine feel about the person she is writing to?
- What words in the document reveal her feelings?

Once the pupils have fed back their ideas, reveal the provenance of the letter and what happened to Catherine. Encourage pupils to think about Catherine's actions. Why do they think she took such a big risk in writing to Thomas? What do they think about her choices? What other documents might give us a different perspective of these events?

Teaching tip

Give the pupils time to look at the original copy of the letter before giving them the transcript. Explain that they don't need to be able to read every word but they should treat the activity more like a treasure hunt for words or letters they can make out.

Taking it further

The pupils could write their own letters to Catherine, giving her advice about what to do.

Spying on a spy

'What can a training report reveal about the qualities needed in a spy?'

Reports can provide fascinating insights into people's characters and events. This activity uses a finishing report for Special Operations Executive Noor Khan. There are a number of conflicting views evident in this one report, as can be seen from the typed comments and additional handwritten notes that were added later.

Print out copies of the report or project it on a whiteboard. Ask the pupils to take just one minute to look at the document. What type of document do they think it is? Can they see a date? Is there anything else that has caught their attention?

Explain that this is a report (a bit like a school report) for a lady called Noor Khan. Do not reveal anything else about the document, but explain to the pupils that they are going to have to work out the rest of this document together.

Now divide the class into pairs and set them on a 'mini-mission'. Can they find the answers to the following questions?

- What skills/abilities are being commented on?
- Draw attention to the codes section 'envelope opening'. What does this mean? Why is Noor Khan being trained to do this?
- What is the significance of the date?
- How many people have contributed to this report? Do the contributors agree about Noor Khan's qualities? Give evidence for your answer. Why do you think they disagree?

After 15 minutes, bring the class back together and listen to some of their ideas and

suggestions. Explain that this is the SOE (Special Operations Executive) final training report for Noor Inyat Khan.

The SOE was set up by the government during war time to train and operate secret agents for missions in enemy territory. Noor Khan was the first female wireless operator to be sent out to help the resistance movement in France. Very few SOE agents have divided opinion as much as Noor Khan. From the moment of her initial training as an SOE agent, her suitability for the role was thrown into question, as the finishing report suggests, although there were those, such as Maurice Buckmaster (head of the French section), who staunchly defended her abilities as an agent. Even today historians have been divided in their assessment of her.

Taking it further

The children could go on to find out more about Noor Khan and how she was posthumously awarded the George Cross for outstanding bravery, in spite of the divided opinion evident in her final training report. The concept of different perspectives and opinions evident in this document could also be discussed. The children could find out more about the role of the SOE, the training they carried out, and about other spies who operated during the Second World War, by visiting The National Archives Education web resources at: www. nationalarchives.gov.uk/ education/worldwar2/ index-of-resources/ western-europe/ resistance/.

A desperate plea

'What can a personal letter from a princess reveal about the game of thrones?'

The source for this activity is a letter sent by Princess Elizabeth (later Elizabeth I) to her sister Mary I. It provides a wonderful insight into the thoughts and feelings of Elizabeth at one of the most dangerous times in her young life.

Teaching tip

You could cut part of the letter into sections and ask the pupils to piece it together in the right order, before introducing them to the document as a whole. This would encourage them to focus not just on the syntax of the document but the content too.

Taking it further

Mary never replied to this letter but the pupils could write their own responses. What might Mary have said? How do they think she felt about her sister's actions and supposed involvement in the plot to depose her?

Distribute copies of the document or display it on a whiteboard. Don't say anything about the document at this point. Just give the pupils a couple of minutes to look at the document and to make some quick, general observations. What do they notice? How has the document been produced? Do they have any ideas as to the type of document it is? Can they suggest when it might have been written? Take all answers as plausible and write them on the whiteboard.

Now give the pupils copies of the letter to look at in pairs. Ask them just to look at the first part of the letter. They should start to have a go at reading the document and see if they can answer the following questions:

- What does the layout reveal about the type of document and the date?
- Can they read any words? What could these reveal about the content of the document?

Distribute the second half of the letter. Again ask the pupils to have a go at reading this part of the document and see if they can answer this next set of questions:

- What suggests that this is a letter?
- Who is it from and who might it be to?
- Do they think that Elizabeth was a queen at the time she wrote it? Why or why not?
- Why are there lines across the bottom of the page? What do these reveal about Elizabeth's feelings at the time?

Ask the class to feed back their ideas and then give them a copy of the transcript to read in pairs. (You could use the simplified transcript at this point if it's more accessible to the pupils.) Now what do they think the document is? Can they date it? Who has written it and why?

Explain that this letter was written by Princess Elizabeth, four years before she becomes Queen Elizabeth I of England. At this point her sister Mary I was queen. Elizabeth had been arrested a month before this letter was written, accused of taking part in the Wyatt Rebellion – a plot to remove Mary as queen and put Elizabeth in her place. Although no conclusive evidence of Elizabeth's involvement had been uncovered, it was decided that to move her to the Tower of London would provide a more 'intimidating' environment.

Elizabeth wrote this letter in the hope it would encourage Mary to reconsider her decision to send her to the Tower. She took so long to write it that she managed to delay her journey by one day. Elizabeth claims that she is Mary's 'most faithful subject' and has done absolutely nothing wrong.

Official letters and records

Part 4

Why was an eleven-year-old sent to prison?

'Crime sheets offer a window into the reality of some children's lives in the Victorian period.'

Photographs offer an instant way to get children to engage with real people's lives. This activity uses a Victorian crime sheet. Authorities at the time started to take photographs to try to record a typical criminal type.

Use this crime sheet: Crime sheet for John Greening, 31 May 1873. To establish the idea that we can find out things from photographs and to get children practised in looking, start this activity by sharing different photographs in groups and let children talk about what they can see in the photographs. Photographs can be a wide selection from magazines, books, old school class photographs and some provided by the children themselves.

Print out copies of the crime sheet or project it on a whiteboard. Encourage pupils to make observational comments based on who and what they see. Why might the photograph have been taken? What was the point of the number? Ask them to describe the boy in the photograph. How is he dressed? How old does he look?

Then ask the pupils to try to read the accompanying writing, using the transcript if necessary. Explain the shortened words like 'Stg.' (stealing) and 'Cal moth' (calendar month). What has John Greening done?

Then encourage pupils to interpret the source more deeply. Why has this information been recorded? Who could have wanted this information?

SOS

'What can a telegram reveal about the Titanic's final moments?'

The telegram, a bit like a text message today, provided an extremely quick way of communicating with others at a distance. The document used in this idea gives us a rare insight into the Titanic's final hours.

Display the document on the whiteboard and, using the spotlight tool or similar, focus on the section referencing *SOS*. Ask pupils what they think this means. In what type of situation might this be used? Now move the spotlight to another part of the document – look at the section that says *Radio Telegram*. What does this mean? Explain that a radio telegram was a message sent between two ships at sea, enabling them to communicate. There would be a receiver set (to receive messages) and a transmitter set (to send messages) on board ships that had this technology. Do we use this type of technology today on modern ships? Can this help us date the document? Explain that this type of radio telegram was used from 1900 onwards. Today ships have technology that uses satellite services.

Now focus on the main message of the telegram. What might have happened? Why might a nearby ship need to come quickly? Accept all answers as plausible before revealing the entire document. Is there any further information that reveals more? Draw their attention to the name of the ship in distress – Titanic. Do the pupils know what happened to the Titanic and why she was sinking? Explain that this was just one of a number of telegrams the Titanic sent to different ships that were close enough to receive them. Unfortunately, none of the ships was able to reach the Titanic before she sank. Many people lost their lives.

On the register

'What can a mill time book tell us about the children who worked there?'

The source used in this activity is a great 'mystery' document (see Idea 1) to introduce pupils to Victorian childhood. It details the working hours of different children labouring at Ramsden cotton mill in Rochdale, in the mid-19th century.

Teaching tip

You could black out the column that mentions the children's ages when you first introduce pupils to the document, and ask them to guess the ages of the people working these long hours. You could then reveal that they are looking at the hours worked by children! This could be a powerful way to draw comparisons with childhood today.

Taking it further

Pupils could investigate other types of employment for children in Victorian times, along with some of the reforms that were brought in to improve conditions for working children.

Show the pupils the document on the whiteboard and ask them for their first impressions. What can they see? Encourage them to examine the document as an object as they feed back their observations. How does the document appear on the page? How is the information set out? Can they spot any words or numbers? Do they have any ideas what the document might be about?

Now give the pupils copies of the document to look at in pairs. This could be done as a class activity on the carpet or the pupils could be sent back to their tables to look more closely at the facsimile. This time encourage them to look very carefully at the document. What can they see? Can they spot any abbreviations? What might these stand for? Who do they think the people listed in the document are? What do all of the numbers relate to? Once the pupils have had ten minutes to look at the document, bring the class back together to feed back.

Encourage the pupils to put forward their ideas. Can they answer some of the 'w' questions based on their observations? E.g. *What* does the document tell us? *When* do they think it was made? *Who* is the document about? Encourage the pupils to explain why they have come to these conclusions. Is there anything that they have found particularly surprising or interesting? Why? Accept all answers as plausible at this stage.

Explain to the pupils that this is a factory logbook for Ramsden Cotton Mill in Lancashire (now part of Greater Manchester) in 1836. At this time, many children had to go out to work to earn wages to help support their families, and one source of employment for children was the growing number of factories that spun cotton into thread. Ask the pupils why the factory owners might have employed children. Explain that children were cheaper to employ than adults. They were also smaller so could be used to carry out jobs that involved crawling in-between the machinery as 'scavengers', or piecing together the broken cotton threads as 'piecers'.

Ask the pupils how old the children had to be to work in the factories. Draw their attention back to the logbook. How old is the youngest child mentioned? Explain that children could be working at even younger ages than this (records include children as young as six years of age). How long are these children working in a day? A week? You could help the pupils make comparisons with the number of hours they spend at school and the number of hours that a full-time employee today might work. Would they like to have been a child working in a Victorian factory? Why, or why not?

Look what came in the post!

'Don't be put off from using official letters as sources in the history classroom.'

This activity focuses on letters as sources for the past. Working with letters can help learners develop confidence in their reading and writing. This particular letter concerns overcrowding in a cholera hospital in Gateshead.

This official handwritten letter, dated 1832, was sent from the Central Board of Health in London to the Board of Health for Newcastle concerning conditions in Gateshead Hospital, which was under its control.

Print out copies of the letter or project it on a whiteboard. Look at the letter together with the class and, if possible, annotate it on the whiteboard. Is there an address? Who is it to and from? Why does it start with 'Sir'? What does this mean? Does it tell you anything about the type of letter it is? (Formal, serious, addressing a government official) What is the date? Why is it handwritten? Does that tell us anything? Define and underline key difficult words, e.g. inadequate, improper, temporary, appropriated, relief, cholera, and so on.

Read through the letter and work out together what it is about. What does it reveal about health in the 19th century? (Cholera spread rapidly; special hospitals were set up to deal with large numbers of cases; there were not enough beds for children.) What is the tone of the letter? Is it angry, formal or happy? What other sources about public health in Victorian cities would help us find out more?

It's official!

'Official letters are not as difficult as you think.'

This activity uses a letter as evidence for the past and can help pupils appreciate the difference between official and private letters. The source is an official letter from the British Foreign Office, which dealt with relations with other countries. The letter concerns Kindertransport, a scheme set up to rescue nearly 10,000 predominantly Jewish children from Nazi persecution. These children left their homes and arrived in Britain from December 1938 to September 1939. Transports ceased with the start of the Second World War.

Project the letter on a whiteboard. Look at the letter together with the class and annotate it on the whiteboard. Where is the address? Who is it to and from? Can you tell anything about the type of letter it is? (Formal, serious, one government official writing to another) What is the date? What could the stamp and numbers mean that appear on the letter? (Letter was kept by the government, numbered for reference)

Now consider what the letter is about. Define and underline key difficult words, e.g. refugee, Inter-Aid Committee. Read through the letter and work out the meaning together. What does it reveal about Jewish children from Germany? Why was this letter written from the British Foreign Office to an official in Holland? How difficult would it be for the children and their families to be separated in this way? You could use a map to show the journey that the children would have taken to help clarify the content of the letter.

Taking it further

Have a look at some of the documents and photographs in the Kindertransport document collection on The National Archives Education website: www.nationalarchives.gov.uk/education/resources/kindertransport/.

51

A snapshot of a football hero

'What can a soldier's war record reveal?'

This document activity provides information about Walter Tull and the two very different roles he performed during his life.

Display the photograph on the whiteboard and ask pupils to make observations about it. What can they see? Annotate the photograph by labelling everything that they mention, e.g. crowd of people, man holding a football, etc. Encourage them to observe as many details as possible, including the different types of clothing that the people are wearing, what they can see in the foreground and the background of the photograph, and so on.

Now take a different-coloured pen and ask the pupils to start making inferences about the photograph, based on their observations. For example, 'I think that the men in the centre of the photograph are part of a team as they are all wearing the same uniform.' Again, encourage the pupils to make as many inferences as possible. Based on their observations, can they make inferences about the date of the photograph and why they think it was taken? Do they have any questions that they would like to ask about the document? Make a list of their questions in a different-coloured pen. How could they go about finding answers to some of these questions?

Draw their attention to Walter Tull sitting fourth from the left in the front row of the photograph. Explain the provenance of the photograph and the fact that Walter Tull was a professional footballer of Afro-Caribbean descent (his father was Barbadian and his mother from Kent in England), who played in the top division of the football league in the early 1900s. This photograph shows him when he was playing for the first division team of Tottenham Hotspur in 1909. This was significant, as it made him only the second professional black player in the Football League. He was a very good player, yet he received racial abuse from some of the people watching the football matches.

Now explain to the pupils that they are going to find out about another aspect of Walter Tull's life. Set them a mini-mission, by asking them to work in pairs or small groups and giving them printed copies of the document. Ask them to find out the following information from the document:

- What was Walter Tull's full name?
- When was he born?
- Was he married?
- What type of job do they think Walter had when this document was made? Why do they think this?

Bring the pupils back together and discuss their findings. Explain that when the First World War broke out in 1914, Walter gave up football to join the army. He was made an officer and this document tells us about this. Draw the pupils' attention to the title of the document and the phrase 'temporary commission'. As the war progressed, more men were needed to fight and therefore more men were needed to take up the senior positions in the army. This enabled men from a wider variety of social backgrounds to become officers. Walter Tull was made an officer, even though black soldiers were not supposed to become officers in the British Army at this time.

Based on the two documents that they have studied and what they have learnt about Walter Tull, ask pupils to explain why they think he is considered a significant person in history.

Training to be a spy

'How did the government use training materials to prepare a spy for their work?'

This activity illustrates the role of spies during the Second World War and some of the ways in which they were taught to master the 'art' of disguise!

Show the pupils the document on the whiteboard (but with the title blacked out). Give them 30 seconds to scan the document before removing it from the screen. What did they see? Did they spot anything about the way the document was set out on the page, e.g. bullet points, underlined subtitles? How was it produced? Did they spot any words? When do they think it was made? What could it be about?

Now show the document again. Keep it displayed on the board and also give pairs a copy of the document to study more closely (again with the title blacked out). Give them five to ten minutes to look through the document. Encourage them to skim-read the document, underlining words and phrases that can tell us something about the document's provenance. You could provide them with mini-mission sheets or chat cards (see Idea 3) at this point to encourage them to pull out key pieces of information, e.g. What did they miss the first time they looked? Is there any information that can indicate when this document was produced? (References to cigarettes, watches, socks) What do they think it could be about? Why do they think it has been created?

Get the pupils to feed back their ideas, using the large image on the whiteboard to annotate and highlight their inferences as they discuss what they have observed. Take ideas about what they think the document is, and why they have reached these conclusions. Accept all suggestions as plausible, before revealing the blacked-out title at the top of the document. Now what do the pupils think the document could be? Why would this type of document have been produced? When would it have been produced?

Explain that the document comes from the special training programme that was used at SOE (Special Operations Executive) training schools. These were places that taught agents (spies) how to behave and operate in countries occupied by the enemy. The SOE was set up by Prime Minister Winston Churchill during the Second World War, so that agents could go into occupied countries to find out information, attack important targets and spread propaganda. This document was taken from the training programme that taught agents to use disguise effectively.

As a class, get the pupils to decide on five of the most important rules of disguise for spies (taken from the original document) and encourage them to write these out clearly and simply in bullet form. Why have they chosen these particular points? Is there any additional information that they think should be added (and wasn't included on the original document)? Why do they think this?

Pupils can then go on to create their own posters as *aide-memories* for would-be spies learning about the art of disguise.

Bonus idea ★

Pupils could investigate some of the other spy training materials available. What do these reveal about the work of SOE agents and the dangers they faced?

Flying high

'What can an application for a pilot's licence reveal?'

This activity provides insight into the life of Amy Johnson and why she was such a significant woman in aviation history.

Taking it further

Pupils could investigate other significant women (using Ideas 30, 31 and 41 in this book) and design their own fact files on their chosen person.

Show the pupils the source document on the whiteboard. Ask for their initial observations about how it is set out on the page, e.g. printed text, handwritten text, sections of the document struck through. Based on their initial observations, have the pupils any idea about what type of document they're looking at? You could talk about how the combination of text and handwriting could suggest it's a formal document and how the spaces suggest it is requesting information.

Now ask the pupils to focus on what the writing says. You could hand out printed copies of the document at this stage. Set them a mini-mission in pairs: Can they find a name? A date? What do they think the document was used for?

Encourage the pupils to feed back their ideas as a group. Explain that this was an application form requesting a pilot's licence. Amy Johnson is the person applying for the licence. When is she applying? Help the pupils understand the difference between the two dates on the form: Amy's birth date and the date of her application. Would it have been usual for a woman to apply for a pilot's licence at this time?

Explain that Amy Johnson was subsequently granted her licence. In 1930, the year after she gained her pilot's certificate, she became the first woman to fly solo from England to Australia. Her plane, a Gypsy Moth, was called Jason. At this time, most female pilots came from aristocratic backgrounds, whereas Amy came from a middle-class family in Yorkshire.

Using a source on the moon!

'A Foreign Office telegram can show history being made.'

Official telegrams are really appealing sources to use in the classroom. They are often fairly brief and by their very nature can convey a sense of importance or urgency, which can add to our interpretation if we read carefully.

Use this telegram: Telegram from the Foreign and Commonwealth Office to Washington, July 1969. This is a *FLASH* telegram, meaning it required an immediate reply. It was sent in '*Cypher/Cat. A'*, i.e. code, so we are looking at a translation of that code. '*RESTRICTED'* meant the telegram was only to be seen by those listed here: the American Department, News Department, S & T.D (Science and Technology Department). The extent of circulation was rated: Restricted, Confidential, Secret or Top Secret.

Print out copies of the telegram or project it on a whiteboard. Encourage pupils to look at the terms used in the source before reading the actual text, e.g. *FLASH telegram, Cypher* and *Restricted*. What do these terms tell us about the content? (That it was important information and had to be acted on quickly.)

Read the text. What is the date? What is it about? What have the men done? What is the name of their mission? Why does the British government want to delay its official congratulations to the USA government? Who is the audience for this telegram? (Look at the distribution details at the bottom.) Ask the pupils to draw some conclusions. Why was this seen as an important event? What other sources from the same time would help us find out more on how Britain felt about the moon landings? (Newspapers, TV, news footage, radio recordings, magazines, photographs)

Teaching tip

To get the most from this type of source consider its nature. It has a sense of urgency. It shows the closeness between two countries and reflects the excitement about space travel.

Taking it further

Locate footage of the moon landings through a web search and find out about other missions.

Suffering for suffrage?

'Use this official letter to explore the significance of Emily Davison.'

The activity is suitable for those studying the National Curriculum theme of significant people. Emily Davison was a suffragette who hid overnight in a cupboard in the chapel in the Palace of Westminster to record her residence for the 1911 census as the House of Commons. However, the main event for which she is remembered was when she ran onto the race course at the Epsom Derby in 1913, which resulted in her death.

The source is an official letter from the police at Scotland Yard, London to the government department that deals with the Palace of Westminster and Houses of Parliament. Print out copies of the letter or project a large version of it on a whiteboard. Ask pupils: What are you looking at? What type of letter is this? Can we tell if it is an official or government letter or a personal letter? How do we know? What is the date on the letter? Who is it from? (Look at the top right-hand corner address: it is from the police who are based at New Scotland Yard.)

Now read the letter. Underline any difficult words: Metropolis (London), Police Commissioner (policeman in charge of all the police); Commissioner of His Majesty's Works (person in charge of all the crown's buildings); vestibule (hallway). Where did Emily hide? Why had she hidden herself? How was she discovered? What does this event show about her character and beliefs? Ask the pupils if they can think of any other sources that could help us find out more about the life of Emily Davison. (Census material, police records, film of the Epsom Derby)

Working cats

'Pupils can use Home Office records to find out about the civil service employment opportunities for cats!'

This activity reveals the 'lighter' side to government records, as children find out about Peta, the Home Office cat.

Talk to the pupils about their favourite animals and why. Do any of them have any pets? Can their pets do anything particularly impressive or clever? Explain that animals have been used by humans throughout history to carry out jobs and to help make our lives easier. Ask the pupils to think of any examples where animals have been given specific roles, e.g. horses have been used in warfare; carrier pigeons have been used to convey messages.

Now explain to the pupils that they are going to be given a document all about a particular animal. You are not going to reveal anything else about the document, but are going to give them the opportunity to see what they can find out. Hand out copies of the memo for the pupils to work with in small groups. Can they answer the following questions: Who is the memo from and to? What type of animal do they think Peta is? Why do they think this? Why is the author writing to Peta? What has Peta done that deserves congratulations?

Once the pupils have had to time to complete the activity, bring them back together to feed back their findings. Confirm that Peta is indeed a cat and that she has been given a particularly important job by the government. Do the pupils have any idea what this job might be? Can they think of anything a cat could do that would help the government? Explain that the writer of the memo was a person in America pretending to be a famous cat, Mike the Magic Cat. Why do

Teaching tip

You could turn this into a bigger activity, by resourcing other examples of quirky or unusual jobs that animals have been given, and ask pupils to become 'experts' on their particular example. Their findings can then be shared with the rest of the class in a mini-presentation.

Taking it further

Pupils could design their own job advert for the recruitment of Peta. What skills does the Home Office cat need to have? What are the main requirements of the job?

the pupils think this person wrote the memo to Peta in the first place?

Now explain to the pupils that you're going to give them a second document that will reveal more about Peta the cat and her job. Hand out the article and ask pupils to read the section about Peta. What type of document is this? What does it reveal about Peta and her role in government? Why do you think this was an important job? Why do you think this document about Peta was made?

Explain to the pupils that Peta was the Home Office cat: the official mice-catcher in Whitehall! When she was written about by the press, she became popular and began to receive her own letters and correspondence from across the world!

Posters and cartoons

Part 5

What can a poster tell us?

'Posters as sources are a great window into any period of history.'

This activity uses a poster to introduce the idea of propaganda at a very straightforward level and to explore the technique of persuasive writing. An understanding of both of these elements can help pupils unlock the meaning and value of a source. Like photographs, posters are an important means for developing observational skills, appreciation of the difference between past and present and concepts of similarity and difference.

The poster was produced by the Ministry of Information during the Second World War. Print out copies or project it on a whiteboard. Encourage pupils to make observational comments based on who and what they see, e.g. 'I can see some ghostly hands of a man in uniform holding a British diary.' Also ask them what the text says.

Then encourage pupils to become more analytical in order to make sense of their observations. Does the poster have a message? What do they think of the size of the font used? Is that important? Is the poster trying to persuade you to do something? Get them to draw some conclusions. What does this show about life in Britain during the Second World War?

Pupils can then design a poster to send a 'message' about life in the Second World War. For inspiration, these examples show how life at the home front was affected during the Second World War: http://www. nationalarchives.gov.uk/theartofwar/prop/ home_front.

First World War poster

'Posters are great sources for teaching persuasive writing.'

This activity helps pupils to understand the power of words within a poster source. Like the source shown in Idea 43, this poster is an example of propaganda, but this time from the First World War. It could be used as part of any study in the National Curriculum concerning the theme of commemoration of the First World War.

The poster dates from July 1916 and urged industrial workers to postpone their holidays to help the war effort.

Print out copies of the poster or project it on a whiteboard. Encourage pupils to read the poster. Ask the following questions: Does the poster have a message? Is the poster trying to persuade people to do something? Who is Douglas Haig? (He commanded the British Expeditionary Force on the Western Front from late 1915 until 1918.) Why is he mentioned? What do pupils think of the design? How does it convey its message without pictures? Why are words like 'appeal' and 'nation' used on the poster? What do they think of the different fonts used? Is the colour choice of the poster important? Who is the audience for this poster? What does this show about life in Britain during the First World War?

Teaching tip

Pupils could study other posters from the First World War and see if they convey their messages differently. Use the online collection from the Imperial War Museum for more examples: www.iwm.org.uk/collections.

Taking it further

Redesign this poster using pictures to persuade factory workers to postpone their holidays.

Coughs and sneezes spread diseases!

'How did the government promote good health during the Second World War?'

This activity reveals some of the wartime concerns of the government and how they tried to promote good health on the Home Front.

A handkerchief in time
saves nine
and helps to keep the nation fighting fit
COUGHS and SNEEZES SPREAD DISEASES

Show the pupils the image of the first document (pictured below) on the whiteboard for just one minute. What did they see? Scribe their ideas. Then show the image again and discuss what they initially missed. Now encourage them to make inferences. What type of document is this? Who created it? Who was the intended audience? When was the document created? What is the message of the document? Why was this document created?

Explain to the pupils that during the Second World War, the government was concerned with the health of the nation. Ask pupils why they think this was. In order to promote good health, the government produced posters and information about staying fit and well. These reveal the information the government wanted to convey to people and also the issues that concerned them.

Explain to the pupils that they are now going to explore two further posters that reveal more about health during the Second World War. Ask the pupils to work in small groups and provide them with colour copies of both documents (available on the website). What type of behaviour is each poster promoting? Why are people being encouraged to behave in this way? What does each poster reveal about the government's concerns? How effective are the posters in conveying their message?

Beautiful Britain

'What does a poster reveal about the excitement of rail travel in Victorian times?'

The source in this activity is a beautiful poster showing breath-taking destinations across the British Isles, aimed to appeal to the late-Victorian traveller. This idea focuses both on the map and the surrounding images on the poster, revealing the new-found appeal of rail travel at this time.

Take the different images from around the map and give each group an image to work with. Explain that their image has been taken from a particular collection used in a document. What can they see? Can they find a place name? Does the place look appealing? When do they think the image was drawn? What type of document might their image have been taken from?

Ask the groups to feed back, giving each group 60 seconds to talk about their observations and inferences. Then display the entire document. What do the pupils notice? What does the map show and how are the images of the places connected to the map? When do they think this document was created and what type of document is it? Why has it been created?

Explain to the pupils that the poster was commissioned by the London and North Western Railway Company. It shows their different train routes available across the country. This poster would have been displayed on platforms, in railway carriages and station waiting rooms to promote the appeal of rail travel.

From looking at this poster, what types of activities did people pursue in the late 19th century? Who might have been using trains to travel around at this time and what might they have been using train travel for? (E.g. sightseeing, holidays, business and work)

Kill or cure?

'How did *quack* doctors and the government respond to the outbreak of cholera in the 19th century?'

Cholera was first recorded in England in 1831. Nicknamed the 'Blue Horror', because of the way in which people's skin appeared to turn blue as a result of dehydration, its causes and how to cure it were not understood. A second cholera epidemic struck England in 1848 and the way in which people responded to this disease provides an insight into society at this time.

Teaching tip

Make sure that pupils have a good understanding of what the conditions in Victorian towns were like and how these environments bred disease. You could introduce a Victorian photograph or image here along with sensory items (e.g. smell pot) to set the scene of a Victorian town.

Taking it further

Pupils could use the second source document 'Instructions to visitors to Glasgow in time of Cholera' to find out more about how the government and people reacted to the disease. What actions are being recommended to prevent cholera? Why do you think this is?

Show the pupils the image of the first source document on the whiteboard, with the bottom part of the text removed. Give them a couple of minutes to talk to each other in pairs about what they can see in the image. Then encourage the pupils to feed back their ideas and scribe these around the document image on the whiteboard. What have they observed? Can they now go on to make inferences about the type of document this is? When do they think it was created? If they haven't already referred to the writing at the top of the page, draw the pupils' attention to this. Can they make out what the words say? Does this title provide any further information as to the type of document and the date it was made? At this stage, accept all answers as plausible.

Now give the pupils a copy of the document, including the handwritten text at the bottom of the page. Explain that this will reveal some further information about the document. Ask them to work in pairs for five to ten minutes. Can they work out what any of the words say and what this text is telling us about the document? Provide pupils with a transcript to refer to, once they have had a go at reading the original handwriting.

Bring the class back together and ask them what the text has revealed about the image in the document. Explain (if needed) that this document is a design for an invention called a 'Chemical Sanitary Belt and Cholera Repellant'. People who were worried about catching cholera could purchase one of these belts and would wear it around their stomachs. Before wearing the belt, they would have soaked it in a special liquid. Wearing the cholera belt was claimed to prevent them from catching the disease. Reveal that Thomas Drew was not a medical doctor. Why do the pupils think that people would have bought this design? Do they think it would have worked and prevented people from becoming unwell? When might people have been worried about cholera outbreaks? Can this help us to date the document?

Explain to the pupils that cholera epidemics led the authorities to act on the findings of investigations carried out by people such as Dr John Snow. Snow looked at information related to the deaths of people in Soho and how they were all clustered around a particular water pump. He believed that the disease was carried in water and managed to persuade the Parish to remove the handle of the water pump so that nobody could use it any more. The outbreak ceased and it was subsequently found out that an old sewage cistern had been leaking into the water source used by the pump. Findings like this led to the introduction of the 1848 Public Health Acts. This meant that the Boards of Health for each area had the power to control the water supply and sewage in their districts.

New houses for old!

'Use this poster source to learn about life in 1950s Britain.'

By exploring the content and design of the poster source in this activity, pupils can find out about post-war Britain and the theme of reconstruction.

Use this poster: Poster advertising a new housing estate in Poplar, London, which was a paid attraction as part of the *Festival of Britain* in 1951. Print out copies of the poster or project it on a whiteboard. Ask the pupils what they can see. Read the words on the poster.

- Does the poster have a message? (Look at the caption: *New homes rise from London's ruins...* The hand in the poster suggests a new birth arising from the destruction caused by the bombing in the war. This is a new beginning in housing being offered to the public. The photograph shows how modern the houses looked inside, not an artists' impression. This is to suggest they are real homes.)
- Is the colour choice of the poster important? (Yes, the colour orange for the roof of the house is perhaps used to suggest the sun and stands out against the bright blue sky. This offers a contrast to the black, bombed-out houses pictured at the bottom. This poster is about the future.)
- What about the size of the font used in the poster? Is that important?

Ask the pupils what words could be used to describe the poster. Is it hopeful, happy or sad? Ask them to draw some conclusions: Who is the audience for this poster? What does this source show about life in Britain after the Second World War?

Wings for victory

'How did Winston Churchill show his support for the RAF?'

This activity shows how the government encouraged people to support the war effort at home.

Display the image of the document on the whiteboard and use the spotlight tool to focus on the picture of Winston Churchill. Ask the pupils if they recognise this person and who they think he was. If they're unsure, widen the spotlight tool to receive the text that reads *From the Prime Minister.*

Explain that this is an image of Winston Churchill, Prime Minister of Britain from 1940 until the end of the Second World War. He helped to rally the British people against the Nazis and he led the military planning and decision-making of the war. What type of document do the pupils think this image comes from? Draw the pupils' attention again to *From the Prime Minister* to help them. What types of document are sent *to* someone, *from* someone? Who might Churchill be sending a message to?

Now reveal the rest of the document. Are there any clues as to the content of the message? (E.g. the silhouette images of planes, the term 'Wings') Read the message aloud with the pupils. Who is Winston Churchill appealing to? What does he want people to do? Explain that Wings for Victory was a fundraising campaign and nearly every town across the country had weeks where they were asked to contribute money for a Spitfire, a Wellington or a Lancaster bomber. Ask the pupils why supporting the RAF in this way was so important. Explain that at different points during the war, Britain's RAF had defended the country from invasion.

Four rules for a happy smile

'How did the British government promote good dental hygiene?'

Although free dental treatment was included with the introduction of the NHS in 1948, the most common way to deal with problem teeth was still to remove them and replace them with dentures. Poor diets and lots of sugar meant that the British population's teeth were in a terrible state! A public health campaign was introduced to help people understand the importance of good dental hygiene as the way to prevent problem teeth, and avoid dentures!

Teaching tip

You could always introduce the document in sections, so that the rest of the image is covered. In this way you can encourage pupils to focus on specific images or terms used, e.g. 'Rules for a Happy Smile'.

Taking it further

Pupils could design their own posters to promote good dental hygiene and think of their own catchy slogans. They could also look at examples of other posters used in this book to see how the British government tried to get its different messages across to the public at various points in the past.

Show the pupils the image of the dental poster on the whiteboard. Ask them to make as many observations as they possibly can about the image in 60 seconds. What can they see? What type of document do they think it is? Are there any words or images that catch their eye? When one minute is up, remove the image and take pupils' suggestions. List their ideas on the board, asking them to explain their answers: Why do you think this is a poster? What did you see that has made you think this? Who do you think has made this document? At this point accept all answers as plausible and don't reveal anything further about the document.

Now return the document image to the whiteboard. Provide pupils with printouts of the image and ask them to work in pairs for five minutes on a mini-mission, annotating the document to help them to answer the questions. Can they work out the following?

- What type of document is this?
- Who has created it and who is the intended audience?
- Why has it been created?
- How effective do you think the poster is at conveying its message?

Once the pupils have given their suggestions, explain that you will now reveal the mystery behind the document! Explain that in the 1960s there was a push in public health campaigns to promote the importance of good dental hygiene. With the introduction of the NHS and changes to people's diets, the method of removing rotten teeth and replacing them with dentures (false teeth) was taken over by the promotion of good dental hygiene. People were encouraged to clean their teeth regularly, to avoid sticky, sugary foods and to visit their dentist. This meant that the condition and health of people's teeth began to improve. In the 1930s it was very unusual for anyone over the age of 30 to have their own teeth, but this had changed dramatically by the 1970s when it was far more unusual not to have your own teeth! Talk to the pupils about how we look after our teeth today and how we understand the importance of good dental hygiene.

Waste not a minute!

'Use this poster source to learn about the home front in the Second World War.'

In this activity pupils explore a poster source concerning the home front in the Second World War. The poster uses a particularly powerful combination of image and text to transmit its message.

Explain the concept of the home front, when civilians in Britain were encouraged to support the war effort. Print out copies of the poster or project it on a whiteboard. Ask the pupils what they can see. Read the words on the poster. Define *yield* and *inch* if necessary. Does the poster have a message? Point out the caption: *Yield not an inch! Waste not a minute!* and also *Work fast!* and *Stand fast!* What does this mean? (Workers must work hard in the factories making everything needed for the war; the faster they work, the more weapons, planes, ships and tanks they produce to help win the war. This is symbolised by the hands holding each other, the people of the country at home supporting those who fight in battle.) The wording used in the poster is also important, so point out the play on words with 'FAST'. Here the same word means two different things, as in a pun. You might want to introduce the concept of homographs – words spelt the same that have different meanings.

What words can the pupils use to describe the poster? How does it create a direct or persuasive message? Who is the audience for this poster? Ask the pupils to draw some conclusions: What does this source show about life in Britain during the Second World War? What other types of sources could we look at from the same time to find out more about life on the home front?

A piece of cake?

'Cartoons can be used to encourage critical thinking.'

This activity can be used to show that cartoons are important historical sources too. A cartoon can be a rewarding choice as a 'mystery document' (see Idea 1) to introduce a history topic. Cartoons appear in most newspapers and magazines and reflect views held at the time. Their creators often poke fun at powerful figures or events through caricature, symbolism, irony and satire.

The cartoon for this idea was created by Clive Upton when he worked for the Ministry of Information during the Second World War. It is a comment on the post Second World War economy. So that the British government could rebuild the economy in peacetime, they ordered manufacturers to sell products to other countries. All luxury goods like cars and sewing machines, symbolised by the cake, were to be exported to raise money to buy the raw materials, like coal and oil, that the country needed.

Print out copies of the cartoon or project it on a whiteboard. Encourage pupils to study the cartoon. Make sure they understand the words 'exporter', 'export', 'production'. Read the speech bubbles. Do they understand the message? (Britain needs to work hard to produce more to export.) How does the cartoon try to make its point? Who is the 'mother figure'? (The government) Do the children symbolise anything? (The Nation) What does the cake represent? Why has the artist drawn a cake? Could it be an easy way to explain a difficult idea? Who is the audience for this cartoon? What does this show about life in Britain after the Second World War?

Teaching tip

To establish the idea that we can find out things from cartoons as historical sources, it is helpful to explore the features of a cartoon. Pupils need to understand that cartoons are a form of visual joke and often show their subjects in a humorous, exaggerated way. They are often used to convey a message and we must look at their style and use of caption.

Taking it further

Make a collection of different cartoons from newspapers or magazines today and discuss them.

Don't be foolish!

'Cartoons are great sources for teaching persuasive writing too.'

This activity involves a cartoon that is a good source for finding out about life at home during the Second World War.

The cartoon is by H.M. Bateman and relates to saving fuel during the Second World War. It shows the interior of a factory where a man has left the door open. Print out copies of the cartoon or project it on a whiteboard. Explore with the pupils the features of a cartoon (see Teaching Tip in Idea 52). Explain what puns are and how they might be used to exploit the different possible meanings of a word or the fact that there are words that sound alike but have different meanings.

Encourage pupils to study the cartoon. Ask: Does the cartoon have a message? Is the poster trying to persuade you to do something? Why is the man in blue made to look smaller than the other people? What is the attitude of the three other figures? Can you explain the punchline of the cartoon (foolish and fuel-ish)? You may want to introduce the concept of the homonym.

How is colour used in the cartoon to help deliver the message? (Perhaps red is used to alert danger or maybe, as a whole, red, white and blue are used to encourage people to be patriotic and support the war effort. Who is the audience for this cartoon? What does this show about life in Britain during the Second World War? Can we look at other sources from the same time to find out more about the war effort at home?

Maps and plans

Part 6

Mapping history

'Maps are a great way for children to find their way back to the past.'

This activity uses a medieval map as a source to interest children in the past, removing some of the difficulties of having to read a lot of text. Maps can offer a unique opportunity to explore the idea of change over time, especially if used alongside more recent maps of the same location.

Teaching tip

Ask the pupils to make comparisons between medieval and modern village life.

Taking it further

Compare and contrast the medieval map of Chertsey with a modern Ordnance Survey map of Chertsey. Which parts of medieval Chertsey are still standing today? What buildings do you think are the most important ones in Chertsey today?

The land and buildings on the map belonged to the Benedictine Abbey which created Chertsey in Surrey. The houses represent the village of Laleham. This map was used to settle a dispute between the Abbey and three people who rented lands from the Abbey and this explains why the name of the tenant, size of field and use of land are recorded on the map.

To get children practised in looking, start this activity by sharing different maps in groups and let pupils talk about what they can see. This could include atlases, Ordnance Survey maps, an A-Z map of a major city or tourist maps.

Print out copies of the medieval map or project it on a whiteboard. Encourage pupils to make observational comments: What is this source? What can you see? Can you list the buildings on the map (using the transcript if needed)? Can you describe the buildings? What were they used for? Encourage the pupils to become more analytical in order to make sense of their observations. What is the largest building on the map? Explore what the existence of these buildings reveals. What does the size of the Abbey tell you about religion at this time? How accurate do you think this map is? There are no symbols or scales here, like a modern map. Why might this map have been have created?

Map in hand

'This is a unique map to captivate pupils' curiosity about the Victorians.'

Introducing children to this particular source is intended to *inspire* their curiosity about learning from historical objects. It is one of the most unusual records in The National Archives. It is a design for a fine leather glove that shows the location of the Great Exhibition in Hyde Park in 1851.

Print out copies of the map or project it on a whiteboard. Encourage pupils to make observational comments: What is this source? (Leather glove) What places and roads in London can you spot on the glove? (Kensington Gardens, Hyde Park, St James's Park, Palace Gardens, Regent's Park, Coliseum Theatre, British Museum, St Paul's, Great Exhibition Building, Somerset House, Charing Cross, Cannon Street, Bank, Drury Lane and the River Thames)

Now try to get the pupils thinking more critically. How can we use this source to learn about the Victorians? Why do they think this glove source was made? (E.g. to celebrate the Great Exhibition; as a souvenir) Ask the pupils what else we can learn from it. (E.g. gloves were popular items of dress.) Talk about the glove as a souvenir. Define 'souvenir' and discuss how today we also have souvenirs for popular tourist attractions.

Ask the pupils if there are any difficulties in only using this source to find out about the Great Exhibition. (The map is quite simple. It provides information about the location of the exhibition and maybe the importance of the exhibition and souvenirs. However, we would need to look at other sources to find out what was on show at the Great Exhibition, who visited it, what people thought of it and so on.)

Teaching tip

Stress that the Great Exhibition was a big event in the reign of Queen Victoria. Look at the painting *The Opening of the Great Exhibition by Queen Victoria* by Henry Courtney Selous.

Bonus idea ★

Make a class collection of different souvenirs from historic sites or museums. Write museum labels explaining why the objects are important.

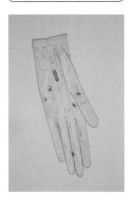

Making sense of maps

'Maps can be an invaluable source for opening the door to learning about the past.'

Maps provide a fascinating way to get children to find out about the past. Just as with any other historical document, maps need to be viewed and analysed with questions about provenance, such as *when* the map was made, *where* and by *whom*. *Why* was it created in the first place? By encouraging children to consider maps in this way and prompting questions about what they can see, they can start to evaluate the map as historical evidence and develop an enquiry-based approach when working with sources.

Print out copies of the top section of the source map (the image of London burning) or display it on a whiteboard. Tell the pupils that this is part of a document. Ask the pupils to spend one minute looking at the image, thinking about what they can see, what might be happening and what type of document it might be. Then ask them to spend a second minute sharing their ideas with the person next to them.

Show the pupils the full image of the map and draw their attention to the image at the top. Now get them to look at the whole document. Ask:

- What can you see? (Record their ideas or highlight the things they notice on the whiteboard.)
- Based on what you've spotted, what type of document do you *now* think this is?
- Where is it a map of? How do you know?
- Do you think this is a modern map of London? Why or why not?
- What do you notice about the map and the different shading? What do you think this tells us?
- What has this map got to do with the picture at the top of the document?

Explain the rest of the detail behind the map. This is a map that was drawn by a man called Wenceslaus Hollar in 1667. King Charles II asked Hollar to create this map to show how much of London had been damaged by the Great Fire of 1666.

Once the pupils understand the provenance of the map, they can spend time studying it in more detail. Set them off on mini-missions to find particular things. Can they find specific landmarks, e.g. The Tower of London and St Paul's Cathedral? Can they spot Pudding Lane where the fire started? What other street names can they find nearby, and what do these reveal about the types of business that were carried out there?

You could also start to get the pupils to consider more about the map and what it reveals about living in London at this time. Can we see any clues that tell us about how people travelled around or buildings and activities that were particularly important to them? What is *not* shown on this map?

Terror in the skies

'What can we learn about the Blitz from a map?'

This activity focuses on a bomb census map compiled in 1940. It is one of many such maps that were used to chart the damage caused during the London Blitz.

Talk to the pupils about different types of maps. What do we use them for? What different types of maps are there? What types of things do they expect to see on a map, e.g. key, grid system, etc.? You could show the pupils a range of different maps to help with discussion and to compare similarities.

Now show the pupils the source map. Ask the pupils about their initial observations. What can they see? Can they spot any place names? Where do they think the map shows? Why might the map have been created? Accept all answers as plausible. Give the pupils further opportunity to study the map, by asking them to work in small groups and providing them with colour copies of the document. Ask them to annotate the map, highlighting their observations. Can they find examples of a type of transport and a well-known building or place? Based on what they have noticed, can they make any inferences about the date of the map? What do they think the coloured dots represent? Once the pupils have had time to make their observations, ask them to return as a class to feed back. Make sure that any inferences they make are tied to their observations.

Once the pupils have fed back their ideas, draw their attention once more to the sequences of coloured dots. Explain that this map was created in 1940. Can the pupils think of any significant events that were taking place at this time? How might these events have had an impact on London? If necessary, help the pupils to make the connection with the Second World War and the Blitz. Why might these events have meant that the government wanted a map of London? What might they have wanted to record on a map of the capital at this time?

Explain that this map is just one of over 650 maps that were made by the British Ministry of Home Security and that they recorded where bombs fell during the Blitz in London. Why do the pupils think the government wanted to record this information? How might it have been useful? Why have they used different colours, dots and circles with crosses? Do the pupils think that they might represent different things about the Blitz?

Explain to the pupils that the different colours represent different days of the week. For example, the site of bombs that fell on a Tuesday were coloured in red. The circles with crosses show unexploded bombs, and bombs that were dropped together (probably from the same aeroplane) are linked together with a line. The diagonal dashed lines show where 'showers' of incendiary bombs were dropped. All of this information helped the government to organise civil defence, as they could study the pattern of air raids and parts of the city that were targeted and damaged.

What's the plan?

'What can we learn about the past from building plans?'

This activity looks at the floor plan for a Victorian school in Shropshire. It can reveal a lot about how children were taught and the subjects they learnt.

Discuss with pupils the layout of their school. What different types of rooms and outdoor spaces are there? What are the spaces used for? What would a plan of their school tell a visitor about the different subjects they study and the ways in which they learn? You could get hold of a plan of your school to help.

Now show the pupils the plan of Quatt School on the whiteboard. Explain that they are taking on the role of a visitor to this school and have to find out as much as possible about the school from studying the plan in small groups. Can they list some of the different rooms and outdoor spaces on the plan? What do they think these were used for? What are the similarities and differences with their own school? What do these observations reveal about Quatt School and the way in which learning was organised?

Ask the pupils to feed back, focusing on the similarities and differences between Quatt School and their own school. Why are there so many differences? When might this plan have been created? Is it showing a school today?

Explain to the children that they are looking at the plan for a school in Shropshire in the late 1800s. Learning was very different then, with boys and girls studying different subjects and working in separate classrooms. They even had separate playgrounds and separate entrances into the school. What can this tell us about the Victorians' ideas of schooling?

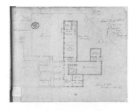

The census

Part 7

Be a census detective (1)

'The census can be used to find out about family life in the past.'

This activity introduces children to the census as a helpful source for information about the past. The census is a count of all the people in the United Kingdom on one particular day, taken every ten years. The first census in Britain was recorded in 1801. There has been one every ten years since, apart from in 1941 due to our involvement in the Second World War.

Use this census page: Census return for Westminster, 1851. This return is for Queen Victoria and her family and useful for those teaching the significant people component of the National Curriculum.

Print out copies of the census page or project it on a whiteboard. Encourage pupils to read it, using the transcript to help. Ask the pupils whose census return is shown here. Who is listed as the head of the household? What is this person's title? Where was this family staying at the time of this census?

Encourage pupils to become more analytical, for example: How many children are listed in this family and what does this tell us about family size? Who else is listed apart from the family? Why are they included? Does this page of the census give us any clues about how the Victorians viewed the role of women? Does anything about this document surprise you?

Be a census detective (2)

'The census can be used to find out how jobs have changed from the past.'

This activity is a follow-up to Idea 59. By studying a different page of the census to the previous idea, but for the *same* area, pupils will learn that the census can be used to find out about different classes of people. They can also compare and contrast different people's lives and see changing patterns of occupation.

After 1851, the age of each person, their relationship within the family (wife, son or daughter), occupation and place of birth were included in the census. The 'Where born' column allows pupils to trace the movement of a family as the return shows where the parents came from and where they were living when their children were born. If all the children were born in the same place it shows the family did not move.

The age column can show how old children were when they started working, how long people worked before they retired and how long people lived. As all the questions are the same, we can easily compare different areas at the same time or over a period of time.

Print out copies of the census page or project it on a whiteboard. Encourage pupils to read it, using the transcript to help. Ask the pupils if they can work out from this census return how Mary Frowde supports herself and her son. What jobs do men do? Are there any jobs that do not exist today? Can you explain why? What different jobs do women on this census return do? Compare this page of the census to the previous one showing Queen Victoria in Idea 59. Can they explain any differences between these areas of Westminster?

No vote, no census...

'How did the suffragettes use the census to promote their cause?'

In 1911, the census survey coincided with the peak of the movement for female suffrage. Women across the country had become suffragettes (this was just *one* part of the movement for female suffrage, as the movement was composed of many different groups). The suffragettes' motto *'Deeds not Words'* signified their support for action, often militant, to promote their cause.

Use these sources: Census defaced by Louisa Burnham and additional page from 1911 census. Give the pupils five minutes to study the additional page in small groups. At this point do not reveal anything about the document, but encourage them to note down their observations and discuss the following questions: Can they find a date for the document? What sort of information is recorded? Who do you think gathered this information and why? Do you have any questions that you'd like to ask about the document?

Now bring the pupils back together to discuss their findings. When answering the above questions, encourage the pupils to support their suggestions using their original observations as evidence. Explain that the document they have been looking at is called a census. The census has been carried out every ten years since 1801 and still takes place today. The only exception was during the Second World War in 1941. It is used by the government to gather information on people living in England and this is then used for statistical purposes.

Explain to the pupils that they are going to look at another page from the same census return of 1911. Show them a large image of the defaced census on the whiteboard. What do they notice? Why do they think the information is missing? Encourage them to have a go at reading the handwritten addition scrawled across the page: *'No Vote No Census. If I am intelligent enough to fill in this census form I can surely make an X on a Ballot Paper.'* Louisa Burnham.

Ask the pupils why they think Louisa hasn't provided the information requested on the census. How do they think she is feeling? Why do they think that she is feeling this way? Explain to the pupils that Louisa was a supporter of the suffragette movement and believed in votes for women. At this time, women did not have the right to vote to have a say in who ran the country. As part of this movement, hundreds of suffragettes took part in a boycott against the 1911 census – they either left their homes for the night of the census count or spoiled their census return papers. Ask the pupils why they think the suffragettes chose to behave in this way and use this type of tactic?

Explain to the pupils that the suffragette movement became increasingly militant in the couple of years following this boycott. They broke windows, damaged property and committed acts of arson. The suffragettes stopped their protesting during the First World War in order to support the war effort. When the war finished, the Representation of the People Act was passed, giving the vote to some women. It wasn't until 1928 that full equality of suffrage was granted for all women.

Taking it further

Ask pupils to investigate the different tactics employed by the suffragettes and consider how effective they were and whether militancy was a help or a hindrance to the cause.

Reports

Part 8

Florence Nightingale's hospital kitchen

'Evidence from Florence Nightingale reveals the state of hospitals in the Crimea.'

This idea is based on a government report used to explore the work of Florence Nightingale and could work for the study of a significant individual.

The source is an extract from the 'Report upon the state of the hospitals of the British army in the Crimea and Scutari, February 1855'. Print out copies of the extract or project it on a whiteboard. Ask pupils the following:

Paragraph 1:

- What did Florence think about the state of the blankets after they had been washed?
- What did she do with them?
- What was wrong with the shirts that were supposed to be clean?

Paragraph 2:

- How did Florence Nightingale try to solve the problem of dirty clothes and bedding?
- What else was done to help the problem of keeping things clean?

Diet table (content):

This table lists extra items of food and drink provided by Florence Nightingale's hospital kitchen. Look through the table together, using the glossary available online to help. Discuss the last columns. One shows the goods provided by the army hospital stores and the other the goods supplied privately by Florence Nightingale. This means she must have raised money privately to pay for these things.

- Are the pupils surprised by anything the soldiers were eating and drinking?
- Would people in hospital eat and drink these things today?

Final paragraphs below table:

- Why did Florence Nightingale still supply goods the army stores already had?
- What item did the government think was not necessary for the soldiers to have in hospital? Why might they have thought this?

What conclusions can we come to about Florence Nightingale's work from this report? (She was highly organised, kept records, raised money to buy things soldiers needed and was taken seriously by government. She must have been a very strong-minded woman, as somebody from her class was expected to marry and not work.)

IDEA 63

Working underground

'What can we learn from a government report about the working conditions for children in the mines?'

Reports are highly structured documents, composed in a specific style in order to present information that has been analysed and considered. This can make them useful primary sources for the historian, but also very dry and difficult to comprehend! This activity demonstrates how the Report of the Children's Employment Commission of 1842, looking at the working conditions in the mines, can be used with a Key Stage 2 group.

Taking it further

Students could investigate other types of work that children had to do in Victorian times. What were conditions like in these roles?

Show pupils the illustration of the trappers on the whiteboard. What do they see? What can they start to infer about the image? When do they think it was drawn? What does it show? Why might it have been created? Explain that the image shows children working as trappers in a Victorian mine. Their job involved opening and closing the doors in the ventilation tunnels for the coal wagons to pass through. Do the pupils think this would have been a pleasant job based on the illustration?

In pairs, now give pupils the extract of John's interview. Encourage them to read through this together, focusing on what they *do* understand. Where was John working? What does he think of his work? What are the conditions like? Feed back as a class, clarifying any terms they don't understand. What type of document might this account and image have come from? Explain that they both come from a report that was carried out in 1842 to investigate working conditions in the mines.

Give each pair the full document with the other children's accounts. Ask them to choose an account and make a mini-report about their chosen child, covering their name, their job, whether they liked their work and anything else they can find out from the account.

Chin up!

'What does a secret report reveal about morale in Britain during the Second World War?'

This activity uses a document that tells us about how the nation's mood was monitored during the Second World War and why the government were so concerned about the issue of 'morale'.

Discuss with pupils the Second World War's impact on civilians and the home front. Explain that the government were increasingly concerned about the British population's morale. Can any of the pupils define 'morale'? Why was morale back home so important? What were people on the home front doing to contribute to the war effort? Explain that the government were so concerned about the effect morale could have on the country's ability to fight the war that they kept daily records on how events were impacting on the country's mood.

Split the pupils into groups and hand out copies of the document. Can they find a title? What could this mean? Can they find a date? What tells us this was an important and sensitive document? Can the pupils find the name of the department that created the document? What do they think this department was responsible for? What is the mood of the country like at this point?

Now encourage them to read the document more closely. They can work with either the original document or the simplified transcript. Can pupils answer the following? Have there been many bombing raids at this point? Why might this have had a positive effect on morale? What do people think about the air raid sirens? Why might many people be glad that the Prime Minister is planning an offensive (counter-attack)? Gather the class back together to share their findings.

Teaching tip

Introduce this document when pupils have a good understanding about the Second World War and the bombing that took place across the country.

Taking it further

Pupils could find out more about the Battle of Britain or the different jobs people did on the home front.

Seals

Part 9

Royal seal as propaganda?

'Seals are a unique form of evidence to explore.'

This activity uses Elizabeth I's Second Great Seal as evidence for the past. Seals were used to prove that the document came from the person who sent it. The Great Seal belonged to the monarch and meant that a document had the monarch's 'seal of approval' and represented their wishes. The Great Seal showed how the monarch wished to appear to subjects and showed the ruler's responsibilities. Elizabeth I used it to reveal her greatness and capacity to rule. Her seal was an instrument of propaganda.

Teaching tip

Encourage the pupils to draw conclusions. Ask them what attributes they think Elizabeth would want people to associate with her image, e.g. majestic, powerful.

Taking it further

Compare this seal to any of the portraits of Elizabeth I available from the National Portrait Gallery and see how Elizabeth I crafted her own image through portraiture: www.npg.org.uk/collections/search/person/mp01452/queen-elizabeth-i.

Print out copies of the seal from the website or project it on a whiteboard. Explain what a seal was used for. Use simple questions to prompt discussion. Can you find the hands descending from the clouds holding Elizabeth's cape away from her body? What does this suggest? (She has the support of God and appears to have divine-like status.) Can you spot a Tudor Rose (symbol of Tudor dynasty), a shield with the arms of France and England, a harp (symbol of Ireland), a *fleur-de-lys* (symbol of the French monarchy)? Why would Elizabeth want to include these symbols?

Now study the queen's appearance. Can you describe her dress, ruff and hairstyle? She looks like a fashionable Tudor lady. What objects does she hold? (An orb and sceptre) Do you know what they mean? (The orb is a globe with a cross to symbolise the Christian world and the sceptre, or staff, an emblem of rule and authority.) The motto says *Elizabetha Dei Gracia Anglie Francie Et Hibernie Regina Fidei Defensor*, which means 'Elizabeth, by grace of God, Queen of England, France and Ireland, Defender of the Faith'.

Cromwell seals the deal!

'Pupils can explore this seal to find out how the power of the monarchy changed in the middle of the 17th century.'

This activity uses Oliver Cromwell's first Great Seal. The design for both sides of the seal was very different from that of earlier rulers and it gives us clues about how the power of the monarchy had changed.

The execution of King Charles I in 1649 was followed by the abolition of the monarchy and the House of Lords. Until 1653, the remaining parliament ruled a republic called the Commonwealth of England, Wales, Ireland and, by 1651, Scotland. Print out copies of both sides of the seal or project them on a whiteboard. Explain what a seal was used for (see Idea 65).

What does the first side of the seal (pictured) reveal? Usually earlier seals show the king in armour on a horse, looking like a soldier. What do we see here? (Map of England and Ireland without Scotland. At the top of the seal is a shield with the cross of St George to represent the arms of England. At the bottom is a shield with a harp to represent Ireland. Ships representing the fleet are shown. The legend reads: 'The Great Seale of England, 1648'. Cromwell wanted the union of England and Ireland. Scotland was added afterwards.)

Encourage pupils to comment on the imagery on the reverse (available online). (A view of the inside of the House of Commons in session) What would it have shown in earlier times? (The monarch on a throne) The motto says: *In the first yeare of Freedome, by God's blessing restored 1648*. What does this mean? (This is a new time without a king and this reflects God's wishes.) What did Cromwell want to show? (Power was shared with people; matters were discussed before laws were made; monarchy had ended.)

Taking it further

Download the free illustrated educational booklet for primary school children learning about Parliament and law-making: www.parliament.uk/education/teaching-resources-lesson-plans/ks1-publication/.

© Shaftesbury Archives

What do seals reveal?

'Seals are pictorial signatures.'

This idea uses a seal to investigate what seals can reveal about the people who owned them.

Use Roger de Quincy's seal for this activity. Print out copies of the seal from the website or project it on a whiteboard. Ask the pupils to look at the seal and describe what they can see. What type of document do they think this is? What do they think it was used for? Explain the purpose of a seal (see Idea 65) and then return to the images that Roger de Quincy has chosen for his seal. What do they think Roger de Quincy wanted to tell people using his seal? Who is the lion supposed to represent? Who is the knight supposed to be?

Explain that Roger de Quincy was a baron in the 13th century (a very important person) and that the lion is supposed to represent the king. This seal is saying that Roger de Quincy is not scared of the king and is prepared to stand up to him. Roger de Quincy's father had been one of the barons who had opposed King John in 1215, and Roger is warning the Crown that he too will oppose the monarch if required.

Get the children to think about the images they might use on their own personal seal. What would they choose to represent them? Ask the children to design their own seal and then encourage them to comment on each other's seals and what they reveal about the person who created them. The children could craft their designs in clay.

Property of Her Majesty the Queen in Right of Her Duchy of Lancaster

Manuscripts

Part 10

London's burning!

'Original documents can provide lots of evidence for the past.'

This activity uses an old tax record for August 1666 and is a good way for pupils to find out about the Great Fire of London.

Use this source: Document to show Pudding Lane Hearth Tax: August 1666. The people listed lived in Pudding Lane. The numbers show the amount of hearths (fireplaces) in each person's house. People who owned a house had to pay a hearth tax to the king twice a year of one shilling (five pence) per hearth.

Print out copies of the document or project it on a whiteboard. Explain that this document shows the amount of money people paid for having a fireplace or oven in their home. It was written about two weeks before the Great Fire of London and lists some of the people who lived in Pudding Lane (where it began).

Encourage pupils to try to read the document (using the transcript if needed) and comment on the information. Use simple questions to prompt discussion. Can you find the name of the king's baker? (Thomas Farrinor) How many fireplaces and ovens did he have? How much tax did he have to pay? (Number of hearths and ovens times one shilling) How many different jobs can you find on the list? Can you name them? How many men had houses on the list? How many women had houses on the list? How many houses were empty?

Then encourage pupils to become more analytical to make sense of their observations. Can they explain why fewer women were listed as house owners? Why might people not have owned their own oven? What type of people did have an oven? What does this show about daily life in the 17th century?

A close shave

'How does a Tudor manuscript show King Henry VIII's power?'

This activity examines some extracts from the *Ordinances of Eltham*, a set of court rules for when King Henry VIII stayed at his palace at Eltham. They were compiled by Henry's chief advisor at the time, Cardinal Thomas Wolsey. These specific extracts concern the duties and behaviour of the king's barber and staff in 1526.

Print out copies of the extracts or project them on a whiteboard. Encourage pupils to make observational comments based on what they see. What type of source is this? Can they make out any words? Try 'king', 'barber', 'cards' and 'dyce/dice'. Now use the transcripts to help. How often did the barber visit the king? What tools did he use to help him with his job? What was the punishment for the barber if he mixed with the wrong kind of people? Why do you think that it was important who he mixed with? What were you not allowed to do in the king's chamber? When was the only time you would be allowed to do this? Why do you think it was so important?

Now, from the content, can they tell what type of manuscript it is? (It is one that *sets down rules* about how people should behave towards the king.) Get them to draw some conclusions from this. Does it reveal anything about why the king would want to be treated in this way? (This set of rules made him look more important and kept him separate from people at court. The strict rules about who was allowed to be close to the king and when, the need to be well-behaved and for servants to keep the king's secrets, gave him more power and control.)

Teaching tip

This written manuscript provides a good way into understanding the power of a Tudor monarch. When pupils have grasped the content, encourage them to appreciate the difference between *what* is being said and *why* this content is significant.

The highwayman

'How can government records help to separate the myth from the reality?'

This activity introduces pupils to two types of document, both about Dick Turpin. It can help them to understand the differences between a myth and a historical account.

Use these sources: Cover of Dick Turpin game box and Indictment of Dick Turpin. Show the pupils the game box, blacking out the name 'Dick Turpin', and ask them what they can see. Scribe their observations before encouraging them to make inferences. Who do they think the man in red is? Why is he wearing a mask? Does he appear impressive? Who are the people in the background and what are they trying to do?

Once you've heard the pupils' suggestions, reveal the name 'Dick Turpin'. Do any of the pupils know who Dick Turpin was? Has this changed their original interpretation of the image? What type of document do they think this picture might have come from?

Explain that Dick Turpin was alive in the mid-1700s but that this document was actually made in 1903 (about 150 years after Dick Turpin died). It was the cover to a board game for children. Ask the pupils how Dick Turpin is being portrayed in this image. Does he look like a hero or a villain? Why do the pupils think this?

Explain that by the early 1900s, there were many legends about Dick Turpin. He was described as a daring highwayman who rode a large dark horse called Black Bess. In reality, he had worked as part of a group called the Essex Gang who robbed people in their homes. When the Essex Gang were captured, Turpin escaped and became a highwayman, robbing stagecoaches. He was eventually discovered in Lincolnshire.

Tell the pupils that you are now going to give out another document that can tell us more about Dick Turpin. Explain that they have the image of the document on one side and a simplified transcript on the other side. Divide pupils into small groups and ask them to work out what type of document they think this is, and what it reveals about Turpin's crimes.

Now bring the pupils back together to discuss their findings. Explain that this is an indictment – a document that charges someone with a serious crime. Turpin was executed for the theft of the horses mentioned in the indictment, even though Thomas Creasy had his horses returned to him. Do the pupils think this was a fair punishment for Turpin? Explain that in the 18th century, over 200 crimes were punishable by death and that most of these were crimes against property. Ask the pupils what this tells us about people's attitudes to belongings and property at this time. Why do they think this type of attitude existed?

The price of religion

'What does Henry VIII's image on the Valor Ecclesiasticus reveal about his role as king?'

This activity helps pupils to understand how images were used to portray power, wealth and importance.

Use this source: Title page image, Valor Ecclesiasticus. Display the image on the whiteboard and discuss with the pupils *who* the person is. The pupils will probably quickly identify him as Henry VIII. Then ask them to look very closely at the image to see what else they can see. Use the spotlight tool to take the pupils through each section of the document, focusing on the king himself, followed by the courtiers and finally the images across the top of the page. At each section, ask the pupils to describe what they can see. Ask, for example: How is Henry VIII dressed? Where is he looking? How is he sat? What impression does he give as a king? What are the courtiers doing? How are they dressed? What does this reveal about their relationship and importance in relation to the king? What are the images at the top of the page? Why are they displayed and what do they represent?

Explain to the pupils that this is the title page of a document called the Valor Ecclesiasticus. This was the document that surveyed the value of the property held by the Church in England. The survey was carried out in 1535, the year after the Pope had refused to give Henry VIII a divorce from his first wife Catherine of Aragon and he had made himself Supreme Head of the Church in England. This meant that Henry now had the authority to divorce Catherine and he could also claim the wealth of the Church as his. He sent commissioners to every county in England, Wales and English-controlled parts of

Ireland to find out just how wealthy the Church was. By 1540, the monasteries and religious houses had been closed, enabling him to claim their treasure and assets.

Discuss with the pupils how Henry's image on the opening page of this survey establishes him as a proud, splendid king, firmly in control of his country and the decision that he has made about surveying the Church's wealth. His courtiers have their eyes averted, subservient to their king, whilst at the top of the document the imagery shows us Henry's divine right to rule. Ask the pupils why Henry VIII would have chosen such a powerful image for this document. What message would he have wanted to give people about his decision to act in this way?

What's the use of an inventory?

'Inventories can provide a unique snapshot of an individual.'

This activity uses an inventory from 1651 – a detailed list of the goods and possessions of someone who died. Unlike wills, they do not record land or real estate or include bequests for named people. They may record household goods, farm animals, craft or trade items, or debts due and owed. The value of goods is shown to cover any debts to be paid off. Inventories provide information about domestic life, work or leisure.

Print out copies of the document or project it on a whiteboard. Ask the pupils what the document looks like. (A list with prices) Define *inventory*. Ask the pupils what this person owned when they were alive. (Clue: Why are Holbein, Leonardo and Michelangelo famous?) Explain that £2 in 1651 would be worth well over £200 today. What can you tell about the person from these goods? Inventories were very common documents in 1651. Yet this document would have been very shocking to people. Can you guess why? Explain that this is part of the inventory of the goods of King Charles I. The goods listed were a small part of the king's art collection. Ask the pupils why this would have been shocking in 1651.

Explain that during the period of the English Civil Wars 1642-48, few would have anticipated that the outcome would be the death of the king. The execution of Charles I in 1649 was shocking. Monarchy had been based on the concept of the *Divine Right of Kings,* a belief that the king was answerable to God alone, and it was a sin to rebel against the king. People would have been horrified to think that anyone would dare to go through the king's possessions and make a list of them to be sold.

Where there's a will, there's a way!

'When researching the life of a historical person, a will can be a good place to start.'

This activity looks at a codicil to the will of Sarah Siddons, the popular tragic actress, dated 1831. Wills are useful sources showing family relationships, details about property, debt, domestic arrangements, religious beliefs and education. Use this idea to support the National Curriculum theme of significant people or as part of a study on the history of leisure.

Wills are used to record what should happen to a person's money, possessions and property after death. Without a will, the law decides how the estate is passed on, which might not be in line with the wishes of the deceased. Sometimes a will has a codicil. This is a legal document added to change an earlier will, like this example.

Print out copies of the document or project it on a whiteboard. Ask the pupils what they can see. First of all find these words in the document and define them: *will*, *codicil*, *testament* (last wishes), *executor* (someone who makes sure that things are done according to the wishes of a dead person's will), *Esquire* (sir). Ask the pupils what they notice about the look of this document. Whose will is this? What was the date of her last will? Why has she added this codicil? Who is to receive the inkstand and gloves? Why do you think these things were especially mentioned in the will? What does her daughter receive? What date was the codicil added? Does anything surprise you?

Birth of a king

'What does a Tudor state paper tell us about the struggle for succession?'

Official documents prepared in advance of important occasions can reveal a lot about the hopes and aspirations of monarchs in the early modern period.

Display the document on the whiteboard and ask pupils for their initial observations. Encourage them to look really carefully and explain that you're not asking them to read the document, but just to describe what they can see. (Handwriting, parchment-coloured paper, etc.) Based on their observations, do the pupils have any idea when the document might have been made? Do they think it is a modern document?

Now explain that you're going to give them a challenge! Hand out copies of the document for the pupils to look at in pairs. Can they spot any letters they recognise? Can they spot any words? Can they spot any names? Give them a few minutes to spend looking at the document and encourage them to annotate straight onto the copy. Emphasise again that you are not expecting them to be able to read the entire document, and that in fact even spotting some letters or words could be very tricky, but that they just need to have a go together!

Gather the class back together and get the pupils to feed back anything they have spotted. At this stage accept all answers as plausible and then draw their attention to the title at the top of the page. Can they read the words *Mary the Queen*? Ask the pupils who they think this might be? If the document is about a Queen Mary, when might it have been made?

Explain that this is a Tudor document about Henry VIII's oldest daughter, Mary I (the daughter he had with his first wife, Catherine of Aragon). Lots of professional historians find Tudor documents very difficult to read (so the pupils have done a great job!), but fortunately there are printed transcripts and summaries of many Tudor documents.

Display the simplified transcript on the whiteboard and read aloud with the pupils. What has happened? Why is this such a happy event? If a baby has been born, why hasn't the baby's birth date been included on the document?

Explain to the pupils that Mary I was married to Prince Philip of Spain, and that she believed she was pregnant with a baby. In preparation, she had her clerks prepare lots of documents like the one above that could be completed when the baby arrived and quickly sent out to the different kings and queens across Europe. Why do the pupils think it was so important for the queen to have a baby and in particular a boy?

Explain that sadly Queen Mary was not pregnant after all but actually very unwell. She never had a child to pass the throne to and when she died her younger sister Elizabeth (Elizabeth I) became queen.

Will he or won't he?

'What can a royal will reveal about the battle of succession?'

Wills are used to state what will happen to a person's possessions when they die and who will inherit. In the case of a royal will, succession to the throne was not regulated by Parliament until the late 17th century. During the reign of Henry VIII, the king could nominate his heirs to the throne through *Letters Patent*, which were published written orders, or by his will in writing.

Teaching tip

This document would work well once the children have some understanding of Henry VIII's life and marriages, his concern over who would inherit the throne and the different Acts of Succession he passed. Remember, Mary and Elizabeth had been written out of the line of succession and were then not reinstated until the 1544 Act.

This activity looks at the will of Henry VIII. Print out copies of the first page of the will or project it on a whiteboard. Ask the pupils what they can see. Draw their attention to the signature at the top of the page. Can they work out what it says? Who has signed this document? Why? Can they make out any words in the document? What type of document do they think it is? Explain that this is the first page of Henry VIII's will.

Give pupils the simplified transcript of the document. What is Henry VIII saying about who will inherit the crown after he dies? Why is Prince Edward first to become king? What do Mary and Elizabeth both need to do if they want to become the queen of England?

Explain that Henry VIII did not sign this will, but that a dry stamp of his signature was used. This makes indents on the parchment and a scribe traces over the indents with ink – a bit like dot-to-dot! Ask the children to create their own 'dry stamp' template for their names, and see if a friend can join up the dots!

Norman England revealed!

'A lot can be learnt even from a short extract from the Domesday Book!'

This task, based on an extract from the Domesday Book, can be used to teach the significant people aspect of the National Curriculum and how medieval monarchs kept control. It was created in 1086 under orders from King William the Conqueror, who wanted to know how much his kingdom was worth and how much taxation he could raise. The result is a detailed survey of the land held by king and people.

Print out copies of the extract or project it on a whiteboard. Encourage pupils to make observational comments: What colour is the manuscript? Does it look old? Can they read any of it? What language is it written in? (Latin is the language used for government documents.) Take a look at the transcript. Can they recognise the meaning of any of the Latin numerals?

Now ask them to read the simplified transcript. Who held Patcham before and after 1066? Why might the change in ownership of land have helped William to increase his control over the country? How many *hides* did you have to own to pay tax? How many oxen are there in the village? (Each plough needs eight oxen.) How many people live in this village? List the people in the village, from the biggest to smallest landowners. Find two jobs, other than ploughing, that are mentioned. What was the value of the land when William the Conqueror became king in 1066? What had happened to its value by 1086? Why do you think William the Conqueror wanted to know the value of the land?

Teaching tip

First define the term *hundred*: a measurement of land consisting of 100 hides, a smaller measurement. A hide was supposed to be big enough for a family to grow their own food. The number of hides held was used to decide how much tax a person paid the king. A hide was 120 acres. An acre is about the size of a football pitch.

Taking it further

The pupils could research more about village life in medieval England after the Norman Conquest.

© Alecto Historical Editions

What can an inventory reveal about a king?

'Entertainments using images and symbols can reveal the self-perception of the monarchy.'

This activity uses a Tudor inventory taken from the Office of the Revels to investigate what documents of this nature can reveal about the contemporary perception of monarchy. The Office of the Revels was led by the Master of the Revels, who had responsibility for overseeing royal festivities (known as revels). In Henry VIII's court, this role became increasingly important, as plays, courtly masques and shows grew in popularity. The Master of the Revels would audition companies for performances before the king and kept an official book that documented preparations for each entertainment.

Teaching tip

Before starting the activity, you could ask pupils to compile a list of qualities that *they* think a good king or queen should have. Why have they chosen these qualities? At the end of the activity, consider the qualities that Henry deemed important (as conveyed by the inventory) and compare it with the pupils' original list. Are there any differences? How can we explain these?

Project the inventory on a whiteboard. As a whole-group activity, ask the pupils to look at the image for ten seconds. Remove the image. What did they notice? What do they think the document might be? Show them the document image again and give them longer to study it. What did they miss the first time? Are there any words that they recognise? What type of document do they think it might be now that they've had longer to study it?

Explain that this document is an inventory (a type of list) taken from the Office of the Revels. Refer to the word 'Item' that is repeated on every line down the left-hand side of the page. This refers to different things that were required for a particular type of entertainment in Henry VIII's court. Ask the pupils to make out the title of the page and draw their attention to the term 'Tourney'. What do they think this means? Guide pupils towards the term 'tournament' and the types of sport that Henry VIII enjoyed.

Explain that this document lists the items required for a medieval joust. When the king was involved in a jousting tournament, the king's horse would wear a brightly coloured cloak called a caparison. This cloak would be embroidered with lots of different images. Each image had a meaning and showed people the types of qualities Henry believed he possessed as a great king.

Divide the class into small groups. Give out copies of the document with different words highlighted (the words represent different images displayed on the caparison). Each group needs to try to work out what their highlighted word says. They then need to consider what their image represented and why this quality would have been important in a king. At the end of the activity, the pupils can feed back about the different images found and the meanings associated with them. What do these reveal about Henry's views of kingship?

Taking it further

Get the children to think about the one quality they think is most important in a medieval monarch. Why have they chosen this quality? Ask them to design an image to represent this quality for their own royal caparison.

What can you find in the kitchen?

'Inventories also capture a lot of information about domestic life in the past.'

This idea is based on a single page from the inventory for the home of James Butcher, who lived in Westminster, which gives a lot of domestic detail for the 18th century. It is a valuable source for teaching about change beyond living memory. The complete inventory from 1738 listed the contents of all the rooms in his house and included his clothes (as head of the family) and his money.

Print out copies of the inventory or project it on a whiteboard. Explain what an inventory was used for (see Idea 72 for details). Ask the pupils the following questions: What objects were listed for the kitchen? What evidence do these objects provide about life at that time? (Lack of electricity; simple dishes were eaten, for example soup or porridge; the kitchen was locked maybe to keep supplies safe.)

Then ask pupils to find four different types of clothes worn by Mr Butcher. Does the clothing listed give us any idea how clothes were made? (Collars and cuffs were removable to save wear and washing.) Are there any items of clothing that seem unusual today? Is there evidence to suggest that Mr Butcher was fairly well off? (Clothing reflected importance and wealth; he owned expensive buckles for his shoes, brass candle sticks and a writing desk.) The pupils can then write a paragraph on what they have learned about Mr Butcher from the inventory.

The masque of monarchy

'How was Henry VIII entertained?'

This activity uses a Tudor masque taken from the official book of the Master of the Revels (see Idea 77). In Henry VIII's court, plays, courtly masques and shows grew in popularity. The masque was a spectacle often performed at court, with courtiers and even the king taking part. It involved dancing and miming, with actors wearing masks.

Project the first page of the masque on the whiteboard. As a whole-group activity, ask the pupils to look at the layout. How is it set out? Refer to the use of paragraphs and verses. What type of document might it be? Now give the pupils time to study it. What is the title? Can they make out any of the words? Do they understand any of the meaning? Explain the idea of a masque and its role in Henry VIII's court – it would have been performed at court with the intention of showing what a good king Henry VIII made.

Divide the class into four groups. Give each group a copy of a different verse. In ten minutes, can they work out any of the words or what their verse might be saying? Once the children have fed back their initial ideas, give them the transcript of their verse. Ask them to read through it in their group. What do they think their verse is describing?

Bring the whole class back together and get children to read out each verse and discuss its meaning. Explain that this masque is telling the story of Henry VIII, how he came to the throne and what a great king he is. Does Henry sound like a great king in this masque? What does it reveal about how Henry wanted to be viewed? Pupils can then return to their groups and prepare a short mime or act for their verse of the masque.

Illustrations, advertisements, drawings and designs

Part 11

What can we learn from an advertisement?

'Advertising posters can show us how the Victorians enjoyed themselves.'

This task uses an advertising poster as an accessible way to engage pupils in the history of leisure. Posters provide valuable ways to encourage observational skills and the appreciation of the difference between past and present, and similarity and difference.

Use this poster: Morgan's Water Show 1899. Print out copies of the poster or project it on a whiteboard. Encourage pupils to read the poster and ask them: What is the purpose of this poster? What kind of entertainment is shown? Does the poster have a message about the kind of experience on offer? *How* does the poster attempt to encourage people to attend this event? Who is 'king of the waves'? Why is he mentioned on the poster?

Encourage pupils to draw some conclusions: What does this show about entertainment in Victorian England? Can we find other posters from the same time to find out more? Do we have similar shows today?

After the discussion, pupils could look at other examples of advertising posters available online in The National Archives Victorian collection: http://www.nationalarchives.gov.uk/education/resources/selling-the-victorians/.

Image of a king

'What can a plea roll reveal about how Henry VIII wanted to be portrayed?'

This activity uses an image of King Henry VIII taken from an official document to help pupils work out what impression of 'kingship' Henry wanted to make.

Use this source: Henry VIII Plea Roll. Explain to the pupils that they are going to be looking at a mystery document! They are going to use their skills as historians to work out what it is and what it can tell us. Ask them, in groups, to make a list of the questions historians ask when they look at a document for the very first time. Ask the pupils to feed back their ideas and scribe on the board. They should have covered: What type of document is it and what does it tell us? Who made it and who is it about? When, where and why was it created?

Now give the pupils copies of the document to look at in groups. Using their document questions, encourage them to make observations and inferences. Next, project the document on the whiteboard and encourage them to feed back their suggestions to the class. Discuss who the person in the document is and pupils' reasoning behind their interpretations. Draw their attention to the Latin inscription behind the king's head that reveals this image is of Henry VIII. Does it look like other pictures they have seen of the king? How can they explain this difference?

Discuss how Henry VIII came to the throne as a young man and that this image shows him at the beginning of his reign. This helps to account for the differences with later images of the king, whose appearance changed significantly over time. What impression of kingship does Henry give in this image?

Teaching tip

You will need to explain to pupils that a plea roll is a document recording details of law suits or actions in court.

Taking it further

Pupils could look at other images of Henry VIII to discuss how his image changed and also the impression of kingship that each document gives. Are there particular ideals of monarchy that are portrayed in every image?

Seeing is believing...

'What can a Christmas card reveal about life in the trenches?'

This activity uses an image of an official Christmas card to investigate life in the trenches during the First World War.

Give pupils copies of the image but black out the wording at the bottom. In groups, get the pupils to record as many observations as possible around the image. Set a tight time limit to keep them focused. Then give the pupils 60 seconds to take it in turns to come up to the whiteboard, record an observation and pass the pen on to the next pupil. How many observations can they record?

Now ask the pupils to return to their groups and use a different-coloured pen to record their inferences. Get them to focus on: Who is in the picture? How are they feeling? Where are they and what are they doing? When was the image drawn? Why was it created? Remind the pupils to tie their inferences to their earlier observations, so they can explain their ideas using evidence from the image.

Ask the pupils to feed back their suggestions and encourage them to agree or disagree with each other, using evidence from the image. Once you have heard the pupils' feedback, reveal the blacked-out text. How does this change their earlier suggestions, particularly about why it was created?

Clarify with the pupils that this is an image of soldiers in a trench during the First World War and that it was used on Christmas cards sent home by the soldiers. Why do they think this image was used? What impression do we get of life in the trenches? What does this tell us about what the government wanted to convey to civilians about the trenches?

The most wonderful time of the year

'Working with pictures can help pupils to chart change over time.'

This activity uses images from the 19th and 20th centuries. They provide fascinating insights into society: what appealed to people, how they dressed and even how they were expected to behave!

Show the pupils the image 'Christmas in London' on the whiteboard, making sure that the title *Christmas in London, 1905*, has been hidden. What can the pupils see? Scribe as many of their observations as possible. Now encourage them to make inferences based on their observations. Why are all these people gathered together? What are they celebrating? Are they rich or poor? When do pupils think this image was created? Draw their attention to the image of Edward VII. Do pupils have any idea why this image was drawn and the type of document it might have come from? Ensure the pupils bring their inferences back to what they have observed in the image.

Now show pupils the title of the image and explain that this is showing an image of Christmas from 1905 when Edward VII was on the throne. Can they spot any similarities and differences with celebrating Christmas today? Explain that the Edwardians continued a number of Victorian Christmas traditions and also created their own.

Now ask the pupils to work in small groups with two additional documents, 'Barnby's Father Xmas' and 'War Savings Christmas' (available online). Using the same skills of observation and inference, they need to investigate how Christmas was celebrated at different times in the past, and what similarities and differences there are between Christmas then and now.

Teaching tip

During the Edwardian period, Christmas trees became even more popular and were frequently decorated with hand-made decorations. Edwardian homes were often hung with yew, laurel and holly, and Christmas dinner for those who could afford it would have been stuffed goose as opposed to turkey.

Taking it further

You could add a further time period to this activity by using the First World War Christmas card image in Idea 82. Pupils could create their own images of modern-day Christmas celebrations.

121

Image of a queen

'What do official images reveal about Queen Anne?'

A portrait and a seal showing images of Queen Anne are used in this activity to help pupils understand how monarchs created a positive impression.

Show the pupils the portrait first. What can they observe? How is this person dressed? What does this reveal about her wealth and status? Who might she be? When do they think the portrait was painted? Why was it painted? Explain that this portrait shows Queen Anne, who reigned from 1702 to 1714 and was the first monarch to rule *Great Britain*. The Acts of Union were passed when she was queen, uniting England and Scotland into a single kingdom with one parliament. Anne needed to portray an impressive image to her subjects.

Now give pupils copies of the seal and tell them it also portrays Queen Anne. In small groups, ask them what they can observe in this image. What words would they use to describe her? What type of document do they think this is? Bring the pupils back together to discuss their findings. Ask *who* might have seen this image. Why might Anne have wanted them to see her portrayed in a particular way? Explain that this second image comes from Anne's Great Seal, used to authenticate official documents. What do the images have in common? What can they tell us about how Anne wanted to be viewed? Explain that some of Anne's contemporaries described her in unflattering terms: very overweight, her skin red and spotted, and her clothing mismatched and untidy. Why do the pupils think these accounts and the images in the documents don't match? Who might have written these accounts, and why?

Thunderbirds are go!

'What can a design for a toy reveal about childhood in the 1960s?'

The items that people buy can reveal a lot about society's likes and interests. This activity uses a design for a toy to help pupils investigate childhood in the 1960s.

Give the pupils the written section of the document 'Thunderbird 2'. Ask them to work in pairs for five minutes. Can they find the date, the registered design number and the name of the design? What do they think *Registered Design*, *Copyright* and *proprietor* mean?

Ask pupils to feed back their findings. Ask what *type* of document they think this is and *why* it has been created. Explain that when people had ideas for designs (e.g. clothes, toys), they had to submit their design to the Board of Trade to be registered. This prevented others copying or stealing the design. Today, people still need to register their designs with the Intellectual Property Office.

What type of design do the pupils think the model craft is? Think about when this design was created and submitted. Can the pupils draw what they think the design looks like in five minutes? This will reveal how little information is provided on the form. Spend a few minutes looking at their suggestions, before revealing that the form would have been accompanied by a very detailed image of the design.

Show the image of the model craft on the whiteboard. What can the pupils see? Do they recognise it? Explain that this is the registered design for 'Thunderbird 2', a toy relating to a popular 1960s television programme. Have the pupils seen or heard of *Thunderbirds* before? What can it tell us about being a child at this time?

Teaching tip

Show the pupils some clips of *Thunderbirds* on YouTube.

Taking it further

Pupils could design their own toy for a child today, remembering to complete a form of registration for their design!

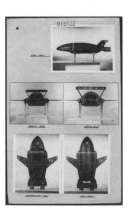

Going to the dogs?

'Advertising posters can also show us how the Edwardians had fun.'

This activity uses an advertising poster to explore the concept of persuasive writing as a means of communication and to learn about different forms of leisure at the start of the 20th century. As sources, advertising posters can be a valuable way to build observational skills.

Use this poster: Rosina Casselli and her midget Chihuahua dogs. Print out copies of the poster or project it on a whiteboard. Encourage pupils to read the poster. Define 'canine' and ask them: What is the purpose of this poster? What kind of entertainment is shown? Does the poster have a message about the kind of entertainment on offer? *How* does the poster attempt to persuade people to attend this event?

You may want to introduce the concept of **figurative language**, namely personification, which is used in this poster. The *dogs* are inviting the audience to come see their show. They mention their *mistress* and even explain how to pronounce their name! How is colour used in the cartoon to help deliver the message?

Ask pupils to draw some conclusions: What does this show about entertainment in Edwardian England? Can we find other posters from the same time to find out more? Do we have similar entertainments nowadays?

Chocolate in the archives

'How can advertisements be used to find out about past societies?'

This activity uses an advertisement for Cadbury's Chocolate to help pupils find out about childhood in the 1900s.

Display the advertisement on the whiteboard, highlighting the girl in red with the spotlight tool. What can the pupils see? Who do they think the girl is? Is she rich or poor? When do they think she was painted? Why might this image have been drawn? Ensure pupils connect their inferences back to their observations.

Widen the spotlight tool slightly to reveal the image of the boy sat beside the girl. Who might he be? Do they still agree with the inferences they made earlier about the girl in red? Highlight what the little boy and girl are holding. What might this be? How can this help us work out why this image was created?

Give pairs a copy of the whole image (with the wording 'Cadbury's Chocolate' blacked out) to study more closely for five minutes. Now can they work out when and why the image was painted, who the children might be and what they're doing? What might the blacked-out section be? Do they notice anything odd about the image? (One of the little boys' heads is missing. The original image is a cardboard cut-out and has been damaged.)

Get the pupils to feed back their ideas before revealing the hidden caption. What does this tell us? Explain that the document comes from a 1900s advertisement for Cadbury's Chocolate. Who might have bought this product? What does the document tell us about childhood at this time? How might it be similar or different from being a child today?

Back to school

'A Victorian school source can be used to teach about changes within living memory.'

This task is based on an image of a school room set up at a home for destitute boys to prevent them becoming beggars or turning to crime. The source is a great way to find out about education in the past.

Teaching tip

Before looking at the source, look around your own classroom and discuss what pupils can see. How is it organised and set up? Talk about what pupils do in their lessons and how they are taught.

Use this illustration: Drawing of a new school room at Regent's Park Road Boys' Home from *The Illustrated London News*, 1870. At this time education was based on the three Rs. Slates were used for young children and pen and ink for older pupils. Wealthy boys were taught by tutors at home and later sent to private boarding schools. Poor children were expected to work for their living from a young age. By 1891 schooling became compulsory.

Print out the picture or project it on a whiteboard. Ask the pupils what they can see. Read the caption underneath. What do you think they might be learning? (Practising to read; reading the Bible possibly) How different is this classroom to your own classroom? Look at the style and layout of the room, type of furniture, equipment, number of teachers, number of pupils, clothing. How do you think these boys were taught? (They had to learn to repeat facts or dates and copy information.) Do you spot the older boy standing at the front? What is he doing? (He was a monitor, an older child who was drilled and then used to help with teaching.) Can we conclude that it looks like a very strict education?

Ask the pupils to draw some more conclusions: Does this source tell us anything about girls? Does this source suggest they were not educated in schools, were taught separately or did not go into homes?

Tyburn's Triple Tree

'What can a picture reveal about how criminals were punished in the 16th century?'

This activity helps pupils to investigate punishment in the 16th century and what this reveals about society's beliefs about crime at the time.

Use this source: Tyburn's Triple Tree. Show the pupils a section of the image on the whiteboard, highlighting the men sitting on top of the structure with the spotlight tool. What can the pupils see? Who do they think these men are? What are they doing? Accept all answers as plausible. Now highlight the crowd. What can the pupils see? Who do they think these people are? Why are they gathered together like this? Now highlight the horse and cart transporting the coffins. What is the horse and cart carrying?

Ask the pupils to think about the three sections of the image and what they've seen. Bringing all of this information together, do they have any ideas about when the image was drawn or what it could be showing?

Now give pupils a copy of the complete image to study in groups. They have five minutes to make a list of anything additional they can observe and to conclude their inferences about what this image reveals. Ask the pupils to feed back their ideas. Draw their attention to the title and the smaller descriptive text at the bottom. Explain that this document shows the permanent gallows at Tyburn (positioned where Marble Arch stands today). Prisoners were transported on a three-mile cart ride from Newgate Prison to Tyburn, with crowds following and then gathering to watch their execution. This type of punishment was used from the 16th century until 1759.

Teaching tip

You could give pupils magnifying sheets or glasses to help focus their observation skills during the group activity.

Taking it further

Pupils could investigate other types of punishment in different time periods (see Idea 32), drawing comparisons between the punishments and what they reveal about society's beliefs and attitudes.

TYBURN'S TRIPLE TREE.

An execution at Tyburn about 1680—From a contemporary print in the Edward Bartley Collection.

Through the keyhole with the Victorians

'Pictures from the past can be used to develop understanding about changes in homes.'

This activity is about looking at homes in the past and exploring how they have changed. Use this illustration from a Victorian furniture catalogue for furnishing a 12-roomed house for £500. This would be approximately £50,000 today.

Print out copies of the picture or project it on a whiteboard. Ask pupils: What are you looking at? Can you spot the wallpaper, screen and desk? What type of person would have used a room like this? Can you give your reasons? What does the term *drawing room* mean? What term would we use today? What would it have been like to use this room? How different is it from a room we might use today? How do you think the furniture and furnishings were made? How is this room heated? How would this room have been cleaned?

Ask the pupils if they can think of any other sources that could help us find out more about Victorian homes. (Census material, photographs, plans and drawings, museum objects)

Ups and Downs of Life

'Have fun with this original idea for a Victorian board game.'

This activity uses another unusual source to focus pupils' enquiry into change and continuity. Pupils could use this source with examples of earlier games from historical periods as part of a study of leisure and entertainment.

The source is a design for a board game called *Ups and Downs of Life.* The images show the cover for the box lid and the board. Unfortunately we do not have the rules of the game.

Print out copies of the images or project them on a whiteboard. Encourage pupils to make observational comments based on what they see, e.g. box lid and board for a game. Study the lid first. What is the game called? What can you see in the picture? How does the picture help you understand what the game is about? Who is meant to play it? How does it make you want to play it? What type of game is this? Look at the board. How do you think you would play this game? Can you think what the rules would be? Can you invent some rules for this board game?

Does this game tell us anything about the Victorians? (They had board games too; they liked having fun and were not that different from us.) Does the game show us anything about Victorian times? (We can see examples of their clothing, transport, punishment in school, their entertainment and sport; they got married and had children.) What other sources would help us find out more about Victorian pastimes and leisure? (Posters advertising events, letters, newspapers, photographs)

Teaching tip

Bring into the class some board games from today.

Taking it further

Compare this particular board game to other games from the past, e.g. Tudor backgammon, nine men's Morris, or chess for the Anglo Saxons.

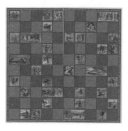

Is chocolate *really* bad for you?

'Pupils can explore the contents of a spy file relating to the invention of a chocolate bomb!'

This document activity uses an unusual invention to reveal how spies might have carried out acts of sabotage during the Second World War.

Use this source: Chocolate Bomb. Show the pupils the first document on the whiteboard, highlighting the illustration for the device. Make sure that the date, title and accompanying text are concealed. Ask the pupils to make some observations. What can they see? Is there anything strange or interesting about the image? Draw their attention to the part where the chocolate is broken. What can they see here? Why is this section labelled with the words 'steel' and 'canvas'? What type of document do they think this image was taken from? Accept all answers as plausible.

Now enlarge the highlighted section to reveal the accompanying text. Invite a pupil to read the text aloud. What does this now reveal about the image? What type of device did the chocolate hide? Why do you think this device would have been invented? Can the pupils think of a specific time when inventors would be encouraged to design devices like this? Again, accept all answers as plausible and don't reveal anything about the document.

Explain to the pupils that they are going to use a second page from the same file to see if they can find out more about the document. Ask the pupils to work in pairs or small groups and give them copies of the second image to annotate. What are their initial observations about this document? Pupils could write or highlight the different things that they can see, e.g. stamped dates, columns. Can they highlight any words or phrases on the document and suggest what they might mean? What do they think this document is and how is it linked to the chocolate image? Do they have any further ideas about the date of the chocolate bomb image and why it was created? Why? Are there any questions they would like to ask about this second document?

Bring the pupils back together and encourage them to feed back their suggestions, annotating a large image of the document on the whiteboard as they give their answers. How has the second document helped them to understand more about the first source?

Explain that the second document was the cover of the file that contained the source about the chocolate bomb. The file is a government document and the reference code KV 4/284 refers to spy files during the Second World War. This file details devices that were used by spies to sabotage places or information in Nazi Germany. At this point you can refer their attention back to the title on the file's cover. Why do the pupils think that these sorts of inventions and devices were seen as important during the Second World War? What other types of sources might tell us more about how spies carried out their work at this time?

Ticket to ride

'Adverts can reveal a lot about the appeal of rail travel in the 19th century.'

This activity uses an advertising image for the Great Northern Railway to help pupils find out about the popularity and appeal of rail travel in the 19th century.

Talk to pupils about forms of transport available today. What do we use different types of transport for? (Work or school, seeing friends and family, leisure activities and holidays) Scribe ideas to return to later. Print copies of the document and the 'layers of meaning' grid (see online resources). Ask the pupils to work in small groups to complete the grid.

Bring the pupils back together to discuss their ideas. What did they see in the document? What are the people doing? When and why do they think the document was created? Explain that the image is a poster advertising travel on the Great Northern Railway. In the late 19th century, the railway became Britain's fastest transport and communication system. For the first time, people were able to take holidays and day trips away from urban areas to the coast and countryside. Ask the pupils how this particular poster might have encouraged people to travel by train. Is it an effective piece of advertising?

Now return to the original list of modes of transport compiled earlier. Run through each type and discuss with pupils whether it was available in the late 19th century. If it was, how might it have differed from today's equivalent? What sorts of activities can we do today, made possible by different types of travel, that wouldn't have been available in the past? How has this impacted on our daily lives?

A funeral fit for a king?

'How much can one picture reveal about Lord Nelson's funeral?'

This document activity uses an image of the funeral barge of Lord Nelson and explores what it reveals about his importance.

Show pupils the document on the whiteboard but conceal the text. What do they see? Scribe their ideas. Now encourage the pupils to make inferences based on their observations, e.g. 'I can see the Union Jack flag, so I think this is a British boat.' Consider what the boat is doing, who the people might be and when the image was created.

Reveal the text. Ask a pupil to read this aloud and encourage pupils to point out any words they don't understand. Highlight these in one colour. Then ask pupils to identify any names and places they recognise and highlight them in a different colour. Finally ask pupils to identify any words that might give us a clue as to what the picture is and highlight these in another colour.

Ask pupils to consider the names and places they've identified. Can any of the pupils tell us more about these people or places? Then ask them to return to the words they think provide clues about the picture. Why have they selected these words? What might they reveal? Finally ask the pupils to make educated guesses about the meanings of the words they don't understand. Explain any meanings they're still unsure about. Now the pupils have looked carefully at the image and text, what do they think this picture reveals? Explain that this is a picture of the funeral barge that was used to transport Nelson's body along the River Thames. Large crowds attended five days of ceremonies, including a grand river ceremony from Greenwich to London. Nelson's coffin was taken on a royal barge.

133

Newspapers and leaflets

Part 12

Yesterday's news is history

'Original newspapers can provide a wealth of information about the past.'

This task is centred on an original newspaper and pupils are encouraged to look at the information contained and draw their own conclusions about the Victorian period. This particular source is a page from *The Graphic* printed in 1884. This was a British weekly illustrated newspaper first published by William Luson Thomas to rival *The Illustrated London News* established in 1842.

Teaching tip

Get pupils thinking about what these advertisements tell us about changes in health, fashion and clothing, or travel. How do they illustrate changes in language? Look at the words bassinette (pram), chronometer (watch), bedstead (bed).

Print out copies of the newspaper page on A3 or project it on a whiteboard. Ask the pupils to work in pairs. Can they find the date of this source? What do all the items printed seem to have in common? (They are all advertisements.) Provide them with a written list of the following quiz questions to answer:

- Can you find an advertisement for toothpaste? How does it differ from today's toothpaste?
- Can you find an advertisement for visiting cards? What are they used for?
- What is a chronometer?
- What can you use to treat a sore throat?
- What does Hagan's Magnolia Balm (cream) promise to do for your skin?
- What can we learn about women's clothing from this paper?
- What is 'The Rover'?
- Can you find a cure for grey hair?
- What is a bassinette?
- Why might people buy Mrs Winslow's soothing syrup?
- How did people light their rooms?
- What is your favourite advertisement and why?
- How useful do you think advertisements are for historians and why?

Remember the Cenotaph

'Newspaper reports can reveal how the First World War was commemorated.'

This activity uses a great newspaper source for teaching the topic of commemoration of the First World War. You may have a local memorial to show pupils or you could mention other memorials at Thiepval in France or the Menin Gate in Ypres, Belgium, for further context.

Use the newspaper page from *The Illustrated London News*, July 1919. Print out copies of the newspaper article or project it on a whiteboard. Read the top caption. Ask pupils: What are you looking at? Explain the term *Cenotaph* from the Greek, which means an empty tomb or monument. Can you spot the guardsmen, General Haig, some flags and a wreath? What is happening in this scene? (It shows the first procession past the Cenotaph, 26 July 1919.)

Does the Cenotaph appear to be a suitable and respectful memorial? Was the ceremony well attended by the British public?

Now read the article below the photograph. A transcript is available online. You could also look at original documents about choosing an inscription for the Cenotaph here:

www.nationalarchives.gov.uk/education/greatwar/g6/cs1/g6cs1s2a.htm

Ask the pupils if they can think of other sources that could help us find out more about commemoration in 1919.

Teaching tip

It would be good to show pupils a photograph of the Cenotaph today and discuss the continued form of commemoration of the First World War.

Taking it further

Carry out Idea 26 on trench warfare using a personal letter from a First World War soldier.

Deeds not words!

'Yesterday's news can reveal a lot about past society.'

Newspapers are a valuable source for historians; they reflect the time period in which they were written and provide an insight into society at a particular time. Yet, like all historical sources, they also need to be treated with caution and their provenance carefully questioned.

Use this source: Advertisements from suffragette newspaper. Give the pupils copies of the advertisements or display them on a whiteboard. Ask them to quickly describe first what they can see and then what they can infer. What type of document are they? What is being advertised? Who might have been interested in these advertisements?

In pairs, now encourage them to look at the document page as a whole – the pupils might have quickly identified these as advertisements, but can they find any further clues as to where the advertisements were published? Can they find a date? Is there any other information on the page that reveals something about the type of document these advertisements came from? Take feedback from the pupils and focus their attention on the title at the top of the page. What type of document do they think *The Suffragette* is? Why do they think this? What do they understand by the term 'suffragette'?

Once the pupils have a clear understanding of what a suffragette was, and the type of document they are looking at, explain a little bit more about the document's provenance. *The Suffragette* was the official newspaper of the Women's Social and Political Union, first published in 1912. It included information about militant activities, as well as other information that might have appealed to its readership. In this way, the newspaper gives us an insight into the types of women who might have supported the movement.

Ask the pupils to look again at the advertisements – what type or class of women might these have appealed to? Can they explain their reasoning using evidence from the advertisements? You can always use an online calculator such as *Measuring Worth* at this point to gauge the value of the items being advertised in today's money.

Once the pupils have drawn conclusions about the readership of the newspaper, can they find anything else on the page that might suggest a different type of readership? Discuss the idea that many historians originally claimed that the suffragettes were supported predominantly by middle- and upper-class women. However, more and more evidence suggests that there was also very strong working-class support for the movement.

Working on the 'Kitchen Front'

'What can government leaflets reveal about rationing and society during the Second World War?'

Rationing began in Britain in January 1940 and soon encompassed popular items such as meat, tea, cheese and eggs. This made the lives of lots of women increasingly difficult; many were working in men's roles and they now also had to feed their families on less food and less variety. The government implemented initiatives to help support and 'inspire' women in the kitchen, including 'Kitchen Front' broadcasts that aired on the radio, recipe booklets and War Cookery Calendars.

Use these sources: Kitchen Front broadcast and War Cookery Leaflet Plan Meals for Children 5-12. Show the image of the Kitchen Front broadcast on the whiteboard. Ask the pupils to focus on the top section of the document. What do they notice? How has the document been produced? Can they see a title and a date? Can they spot a time? What do they think the term 'Kitchen Front' might mean and what might the document be about? Why has a time been included? Can this help us identify what *type* of document this is? Support the pupils' observations by asking them to think about what else is happening for Britain in 1943.

Ask the pupils to now focus on the first paragraph of the document *'Are you ready to take down the recipe?'* Ask a child to read this section of the document aloud. What is the narrator of the document doing? Why might she be passing on a recipe? Who would she be passing this information to? Why are women inventing recipes and sharing them with each other in this way? Explain that this document is a script for a radio programme called the 'Kitchen Front' that was broadcast on the radio every morning. Ask the pupils who they think might have listened to this programme. Why did the government think it was important to have radio broadcasts like this? Do the pupils like the sound of this recipe? Why or why not?

Now explain to the pupils that they are going to look at a second document in small groups and that it will reveal some more information about rationing during the Second World War. Chat cards (see Idea 3) could be used to guide the pupils' observations and inferences. Give them copies of the leaflet and encourage them to scribe their observations on the facsimile of the document. Can the pupils work out: What is the document about? Who has produced it? Why? Who would have been interested in reading this document? Can you find any foods that sound unusual and that you wouldn't see in people's meals today? How are these meals different from the meals that you eat? What sorts of foods are missing? Why do you think this is? Would you like to eat the meals on this menu? Why or why not?

Bring the pupils back together and hear their responses. Explain that women had to be creative with their cooking and use substitutes for some foods that were in short supply, such as eggs and meat. The government was concerned that children should be getting enough food and eating healthy diets, which led them to produce meal planners and guidance for mothers. For some working-class families, rationing actually meant better nutrition at times, e.g. the wide availability of milk and calcium added to flour helped these families consume the recommended intake of calcium. The government's 'Vitamin Welfare' scheme for children, which gave children under five years of age a portion of orange juice every day, is another good example of this.

A spot of light reading

'How can a ladies' almanack from 1740 tell us about womanhood at this time?'

This activity uses a handbook written for ladies, to help pupils find out about the interests and perceptions of women in the 18th century.

Use this source: The Woman's Almanack. Use the spotlight tool to focus on the central figure in the source on the whiteboard. Ask the pupils to describe what they see, then make inferences based on their observations. Who is the figure? (Queen Caroline, married to George II) How is she dressed? When do you think she was drawn? What type of document might this picture have been taken from?

Now widen the spotlight tool so the entire image is visible. Can they spot a title and a date? How has the document been produced? What do they notice about the font? Who do they think this document was aimed at? What is the additional text around the picture about? Why has this been included?

Explain to the pupils that they are looking at the cover of an almanack (a handbook published each year) aimed at women. What do they think might have been inside? By the end of the 1600s publishers had begun to realise that women could form a distinct readership group and the Woman's Almanack was the first of its type. It was aimed at wealthy, educated, literate women. It initially contained flattering poems, romantic stories and recipes, but later editions included mathematical puzzles and riddles, revealing a lot about the women who read this and their interest in popular science. There were blank pages to record baptisms and a list of important dates in the Church of England calendar.

Useful jobs that girls can do

'How were girls encouraged to support the war effort?'

This activity uses a government-produced leaflet to introduce pupils to the concept of 'girls' jobs' during the Second World War.

Talk about the jobs the children do around the house to help their parents. What jobs do their parents do at home? Does one parent take responsibility for certain tasks? Explain that today the roles of men and women (and the jobs they do at home and work) are very flexible.

Show the source on the whiteboard and ask pupils: What can they see? What type of document might this be? When do they think it was made? Who created it and for which audience? What might it be about? Explain that this is a poster made by the Board of Trade during the Second World War to encourage civilians to support the war effort. It is aimed specifically at females and is about the jobs they can do at home. Why would these tasks support Britain at war? Read aloud the first paragraph. Ask for pupils' comments and explain that all of the tasks are about surviving with limited resources and 'make do and mend'; rationing meant a shortage of not only food but lots of other things as well.

Ask the pupils to work in small groups with an enlarged printed copy of the document to find the following: a task that encourages women to make do and mend; a task that would have been seen as 'women's work' at this time; a task that would have been seen as 'men's work'. How effective do the pupils think this document would have been in encouraging and educating women to 'make do and mend' and to assume some of the men's responsibilities around the home?

Teaching tip

You could encourage different groups to focus on different sections of the document, so they are not faced with a large amount of text.

Taking it further

Pupils could find out more about the other roles women took on outside the home during the Second World War. They could make their own posters about 'women's work' based on their findings.

143